# SOCIAL SKILLS FOR KIDS

7 Easy Steps to Help Your Child Build Confidence, Manage Emotions, Make Friends, and Develop Effective Communication Skills

**MICHELLE ADAMS**

# CONTENTS

# INTRODUCTION

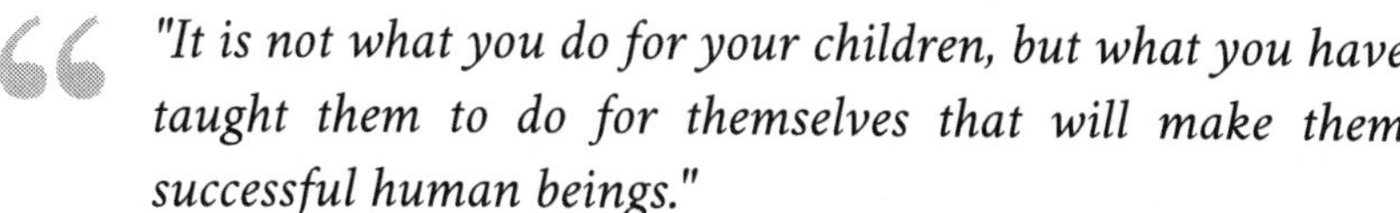

> *"It is not what you do for your children, but what you have taught them to do for themselves that will make them successful human beings."*
>
> — ANN LANDERS

"I sat there for 15 minutes every day, five days a week, and he did not show any interest in joining the other kids. Not once! What am I doing wrong? I don't want my child to be lonely or bullied like I was."

These are the words of one of the many mothers who have made their way to my office over the past couple of years—desperate to get their children the help and support they need to become more socially confident and active. While her story is unique to her, her problems weren't all that different from the many other parents sitting on my couch, doubting their parental skills and abilities. As parents, we tend to always seek within to see where the problem lies because we want our children to be happy. Therefore, the first goal of this book is to put your mind at ease and to help you understand that while you can help your child to become more social, it is not due to poor parenting that your child is facing challenges in this regard. The second goal is to equip you to help your child develop the necessary skills in a fun and engaging manner.

Socializing can be tough for anyone. Even the most extroverted kids will feel shy, uncertain, and out of their depth if they find themselves in a social situation they've never experienced before. Sure, most of us are born with the ability to talk to others, reach out to them, and connect on various levels. We are born with the ability to express emotions, make decisions, and recognize our worth. Socializing is simply a matter of nurturing and improving these abilities. Therefore, I am sharing the necessary tools you can teach your child so that they can master the following skills.

- Seven crucial social skills–and how they're all related.
- How to spot a bully–and get them to stop bothering you.
- How to feel and express emotions in a healthy, non-destructive way.
- How to practice empathy, communication, and smart decision-making.
- How to find and nurture positive, healthy self-esteem.
- How to make friends–and not take it personally if the other child doesn't want to be friends back.
- The hidden power of making choices–and mistakes!

After working for several years with kids of all ages, I know that it is often the case that they are perfectly normal, and they need to be equipped with the right skills to make lasting friendships.

Throughout the book, we will explore kids' different developmental stages, from being mere babies until 10 years and older. We'll look at how these stages impact their behavior, social interaction, and confidence to put themselves out there, be vulnerable and make friends. Every chapter is jam-packed with advice, tips, and games you can play together to prepare them for successful adulthood. This book makes parental support affordable as it is a guide to make parenting a just little easier by offering you a helping hand to become the parent you want to be. It also keeps things easy to remember and easy to reference by keeping the main points at seven skills, seven steps per skill.

So, are you ready to equip yourself with the necessary tools to bring your child out of the desolate shadow of the playground and onto the center stage, surrounded by friends?

Let's jump right in!

1

# HOW DO I MANAGE MY EMOTIONS?

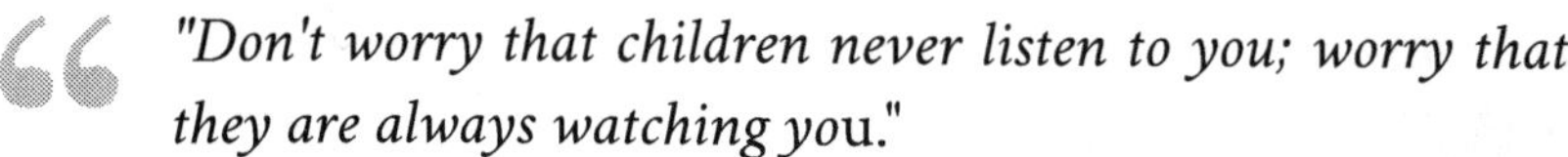

> *"Don't worry that children never listen to you; worry that they are always watching you."*
>
> — ROBERT FULGHUM

One of the key contributing factors when it comes to lacking social skills is the inability to manage emotions effectively. Of course, this is as much true for your child as it is for you. That said, in life—often at work or in traffic—we come across almost as many adults who still struggle to express their emotions accurately and constructively as in the preschool playground. So, can we really blame the preschooler for their poor ability to manage their emotions if we struggle with this ourselves?

Of course not, so let's explore the importance of emotions.

## Control, Don't Suppress

As emotions can be such a sticky toffee to deal with and coupled with the popular belief that expressing emotions puts you in a vulnerable position, it is just far easier to suppress them, right? It may be easier, but it isn't good for you or your child.

Why am I reflecting on your emotional management? Because your child learns a lot from observing you. While this puts immense pressure on you to always behave exemplarily, you can also use this notion to your benefit. Yes, by improving the way you manage your emotions, you are giving your child an example of how to manage theirs much better. Once your child has mastered that, you've laid the foundation for success in the social arena.

By showing our emotions, we provide honest feedback on what we experience. It is a way to communicate to others what we need and guides them on reaching out to us. Our emotions support our survival. For example, fear makes you alert and prepares your body for fight-or-flight mode, the most primal response that has kept humankind alive since our ancestors hunted for food.

When you experience a surge of emotions, instinctively responding can be so easy. Yet, your response should always be guided by the answers to these five questions:

- What am I feeling?
- Why am I experiencing these emotions?
- What should I do with what I am feeling?
- How intense are these feelings?
- What action would justify but not overcompensate for what I am feeling?

When you learn to identify and manage your emotions better, you also identify what others are feeling better. It is also how you learn how to respond appropriately to the display of feelings.

Remember to never confuse emotional management with suppressing what you are feeling. No, emotional management refers to your ability to identify your emotions, acknowledge that you feel them, and respond in an appropriate and socially acceptable manner. It is a way to be authentically you, while it also increases your confidence and self-esteem. All of these contribute to the ease with which you interact socially.

How does all of this help you to help your child? From birth onwards, your babies go through several development stages. In each of these stages, they would have different predominant needs, develop in different areas, and are ready to learn various unique skills linked to the specific stage. So, to understand your child better, I am sharing the different emotional needs children have in every development stage.

### Babies (0-1 Year)

There isn't any need to manage emotions during this life stage. Your baby is also not yet developed to distinguish between different emotions, and they also don't experience the full spectrum of emotions we as adults do. That said, this is a good time to start training your baby to self-soothe.

### What is Self-Soothing?

Self-soothing is the most basic form of emotional regulation and will set the foundation for your child's future emotional management.

## The Benefits of Self-Soothing

When babies learn to self-soothe, they will be able to fall asleep without your help. How often do you find yourself trying to get your baby to sleep, and they wake right up again when you move away from the crib? It can be an extremely frustrating position to be in as you are likely falling behind on chores or missing out on vital sleep while standing on duty at the crib.

But besides enabling your baby to fall asleep by themselves when they wake up in the middle of the night, self-soothing also instills the kind of comfort necessary to have your child play by themselves, content and calmly.

I don't recommend introducing self-soothing until your little one is at least three months old, but there is no need to delay the process any further.

Every baby is a different and unique little person, and while there are certain behaviors you can expect to see in your child, it is also important to always remember there is no one-size-fits-all solution when it comes to raising kids. Therefore, I am sharing seven of the most common steps to help your child switch from always expecting you to comfort them to learning how to calm their own emotions.

### Step 1: Meet Their Needs First

Your baby is not going to be soothed while they experience any physical discomfort. For babies, this discomfort is mostly in the form of a wet or dirty diaper, a hungry belly, too hot or cold, thirst, exposure to too much stimulation, overtired, and gas-causing pain. Only once you've addressed all these concerns can you proceed.

**Step 2: Get the Schedule Right**

Children of all ages thrive once they have a certain routine. Routine is more than just a way to ensure your home runs effectively. No, it also provides your baby security and leaves them feeling safe. Picture living a life in which you have no clue of what is going to happen next while you have no control over anything that happens to you, compared to having the certainty of knowing what is happening next. While time still is irrelevant to your baby, their internal clock is already operational. If you are sticking to a routine of bathing, feeding them at the same time, they are bound to fall into that rhythm, and they'll soon learn when they are about to go to sleep. Try to establish a routine early on in their lives, as this will give your child a sense of security and make life a lot easier for you, too, for years to come.

**Step 3: Comfort/Security Object!**

There is no need to fill their cribs with lots of soft toys, but leaving one soft toy or blanket with them will be helpful, which they will eventually associate with bedtime. Babies form an attachment to such an object, and they find comfort in this connection they've made with that thing.

**Step 4: Keep It Cool & Dark**

When the environment around your child's crib is too light or busy, they will really struggle to sleep. Create a cool and calming environment that is dark enough so that they are not exposed to any distractions that will not help them to fall asleep. If your baby is struggling to fall asleep, it can become as cranky as someone who has insomnia, and then self-soothing becomes unnecessarily hard to achieve.

**Step 5: Stay Close By... Just In Case**

Self-soothing doesn't mean you have to leave your baby crying alone. No, you can still be close by, especially at first, but don't pick them up from the crib. Instead, talk to your baby and give them attention without picking them up. Gradually, they'll learn that it is okay not to be picked up and that they can still feel safe and secure without it.

**Step 6: Try A Pacifier or Swaddle**

A pacifier is a wonderful tool when you are looking for something to soothe your baby, and surely you can use it at times. Just keep in mind that some babies become so attached to their pacifier that it can be very challenging to wean them off this habit at a later stage. The best advice to prevent this from happening is to not always pass the pacifier to them whenever they get upset. No, use this only at certain times, like when it is bedtime or have a nap.

**Step 7: Talk to Baby but Keep Them in The Crib!**

It is common practice for many parents to let their babies fall asleep in their arms. It is just a treat to look at their little faces, but what happens next may be a problem for them and, therefore, also for you. Once your baby is asleep, you carry them to their crib and put them to bed. When they wake up, they are no longer in the same space as where they fell asleep. This can be unsettling, so they cry for you. If you let your baby fall asleep on their own in their beds, they still recognize the place when they wake up, and it is easier for them to fall back to sleep again.

These steps aren't hard to follow, but they can make a huge difference in your life now, as you may buy yourself several more hours of sleep while they'll also help your little one to get better at calming themselves down, which is so important later in life.

### Toddlers (1-3 Years)

Tough times indeed in the parenting years. At this stage, your child is starting to experience several emotions like fear, anger, and happiness. Yet, these are all new sensations to them, and they don't have the vocabulary to express what they experience. As your child is also not old enough yet to sit down and have an honest heart-to-heart conversation, you need to find an alternative way to distract them from the discomfort they are experiencing.

### Can Toddlers Self-Regulate Emotions?

Yes, an effective approach to this challenge is to help them avoid emotionally upsetting situations that can cause them to get angry. If you do end up in such a situation, know that they are still easily distractible, and you can use this to your advantage. Once they become a little older, you can introduce them to the skills necessary to regulate their emotions effectively.

How do you do this? First of all, you need to provide them with a framework that enables them to regulate their emotions. As a parent, a lot of their framework linked to emotional management revolves around you. Therefore, it should come as no surprise that the first step would be called monkey see, monkey do.

### Step 1: Monkey See, Monkey Do

You can tell your child the same thing over 1,000 times and still see no change, but just do or say something inappropriate, and that is what they'll repeat, right? Many parents have learned this lesson in quite embarrassing ways. If you are going to lose your cool and explode verbally when your child is in the vicinity, you can be sure that their eyes are fixated on mommy or daddy, and the next time they get upset, they'll portray the same behavior. It is hard to always remain calm when you feel like you can't bite your lip any longer, but rather use these moments to show your child how to react when upset or sad and let them learn from your example.

**Step 2: What's That Emotion?**

Emotions come with a vocabulary of their own, and what makes it even harder is that you can't explain to your child what every emotion feels like. But when you are sad, and you look sad, talk to your child and say that mommy or daddy is sad, happy, angry, or any other emotion. That is how they will link emotions with the words that describe them.

**Step 3: Name Your Emotion!**

The next stage would be to help your child identify and express their feelings. If you can see they are sad or angry, ask them what they are feeling. Guide them until they get the right word to describe their emotional state. Through regular practice, this becomes easier.

**Step 4: Your Feelings Are Valid**

It is so easy to brush off a child's extreme expression of emotion as nothing to calm them down, but it sets the assumption that their emotions aren't valid. Always ensure your child that what they are feeling is real and important but that there are better ways to express what they are feeling. Don't dismiss the emotion; instead, teach appropriate ways to make others aware of what you are feeling.

**Step 5: Feel, But Don't Act**

Children are not yet capable of expressing different emotions, so they easily confuse every unpleasant emotion with anger. Therefore, many anger tantrums are present so often at this time of their life. While you don't want to dismiss their feelings, you also need to establish ground rules stating in clear terms what are acceptable ways to express anger and what won't be tolerated. This is the time when you should use statements like, "I know you are angry, but I won't let you hurt your sister," or "I can see that you are very sad, but a tantrum is not going to make it any better."

**Step 6: Encourage and Praise: You Did a Good Job!**

It is too easy to focus on the things kids need to do better. Yes, for sure, these are often the times when we are forced to step in but remember to praise your child more often for good behavior than reprimanding them when they behave poorly. I always tell parents to try and to catch their children doing well, and when they do, make sure they know how proud you are of them. Children thrive on attention, and if they don't get positive attention, they will seek the negative. When your child expresses their emotions the way you've taught them, praise them, as you want to reinforce this behavior.

**Step 7: Avoid When All Else Fails**

Certain situations may cause such a severe emotional response in your child that avoiding these situations is really the best solution. Therefore, avoidance or distraction is very much part of the strategies you can employ to strengthen your child's framework for emotional management.

**Preschoolers (3-5 Years)**

Preschoolers thrive on emotions. It is as if their emotions are the fuel to their every action.

Once your child reaches this stage, they are likely to understand what they are feeling but are still completely clueless on how to react to these emotions and don't even have a vague idea yet of what is an acceptable way to express what they are feeling. So how do you approach this situation successfully? Here are the seven steps to guide you.

**Step 1: What's Your Trigger?**

Have you been able to successfully identify your emotional triggers? Now, you can help your child to do the same. We all have these triggers that impact us in a specific way to create an emotional explosion. When your child has calmed down after such an explosion, you can guide them back to the moments before it happened to help them to identify what made them react this way. Repeat this whenever such an outburst occurs, and once you've identified these triggers, you can guide your child on how to avoid them or how to deactivate the button.

**Step 2: Label Your Feelings**

Picture a filing system where you have a load of files, each properly labeled and explaining the contents. Help your child to do the same with their emotions. Label these emotions and link to the label the appropriate response for every emotion. If you can help your child create such a system, it becomes much easier to know how to react whenever a certain emotion is triggered. They just need to revert to the specific file, and they'll know how they can express this emotion. To make it even more real for your child, you can create a pinboard with pictures representing every emotion and what reactions are good and which are not. Remember, there are no bad emotions, only bad responses.

**Step 3: Want to Talk About It?**

Talk to your child when you can see they are upset, or if it is better when they're calmed down, do it then. By discussing their emotions with them, they become more familiar with their feelings and how to express them in acceptable manners. It is also a way to help them understand that it is okay to feel what they do.

**Step 4: Your Feelings Are Valid**

By talking to your child about their emotions, you let them understand what they are feeling is real and valid and that you understand what they go through. It gives your child the certainty that you are there for them, and they can come to you when things are bothering them. This is the first step of creating an open way of communication you want with your child for years to come. It will also help your child to know that what they are feeling is real but that they are strong enough to pull through the situation.

It is best not to dismiss their feelings by telling them something like, "You're okay."; or "There's nothing to be scared of."; or "It will be fine." These types of comments will cause them to think that what they are feeling is wrong, and they will never learn to trust their emotions.

### Step 5: But No Outbursts, Please!

Whatever you do, it is important to always underline that while you respect your child's emotions, you won't tolerate outbursts. Never should it come across as if an explosion can be justified or that poor expression of anger can be excused. Especially if this has been the consistent message in your home for a while already and if you portray acceptable behavior when upset.

### Step 6: Watch Your Parents

This links in with the previous step, and there is only a little more to say on the topic than I already did. However, the reality is that as long as your children depend on you and stay under your roof, they will always observe your behavior and mimic the same.

### Step 7: You Can Learn Healthy Coping!

Your child can learn many different skills to better manage their emotions from a young age onwards. For example, one of the easiest ways they can calm themselves down is through deep breathing exercises. Let them practice this and see how it feels. If exercises like these become a regular activity in your home, it will be much easier for your children to fall back on these ways to overcome emotionally charged moments.

## Elementary Schoolers (5-10 Years) & Middle Schoolers (10+)

Roughly from 5 to 6 years old, children begin to grasp that actions have consequences. It is the developmental stage when they begin to understand that they must look both ways before crossing a street, stop at a stop sign, and never talk to strangers.

Therefore, it is the perfect age to start making them aware of the impact of their actions.

### Step 1: Slow Down and Reflect

While up to now, your child has limited, if any, understanding of the impact their actions have on others when they are reacting with emotional outbursts. But no more. Now their brains have developed enough that you can sit them down and talk about the consequences of their actions.

Did your child hit a sibling? Scream at a stranger? Threw a tantrum in the middle of your local *Target* store? Once they are calm, chat with them about the true impact of their reactions and why it isn't good. Also, look at healthier ways to express their feelings in the future.

### Step 2: Is This Your Trigger?

As your child grows older, they become better at identifying their feelings and can, therefore, better identify what sets them off to feel a certain way in the first place. First, help your child to identify their triggers accurately. Once you do, find ways to avoid these triggers or draft a better response plan to guide your child to better deal with the emotional disturbance.

### Step 3: Talk It Out

You know the value of having a deep heart-to-heart conversation with a friend. Talking to someone about your feelings is an excellent way to process what you are feeling and look at your emotions in a different light.

Give your child the same opportunity and talk to them about their feelings and what caused them to feel a certain way. Such conversations are wonderful opportunities to help them to identify their triggers and to find acceptable ways to express their emotions. It will also help your child feel that their emotions are valid and real.

**Step 4: Are You Sure You Want to Do That?**

Having these conversations with your child is also the time when you can ask questions like the following:

- What do you think is going to happen if you punch your brother?
- How do you think mommy is going to feel if you are rolling on the floor in a tantrum?
- What will happen if you scream at other kids at school?

Essentially, this conversation would happen before your child acts out rather than reflecting on their reaction's impact on others and themselves.

**Step 5: You Can Always Walk Away**

This is such an important lesson that we as adults should also remind ourselves of regularly. Just because poison is served doesn't mean you have to drink it. You always have the choice to walk away from conflict, regardless of whether you are 6 or 60. Explain to your child why walking away is not only, at times, the only thing you can do but also the best thing you can do.

For example, when one of the other kids taunts your child on the school grounds, and they get angry or hurt, it may seem like punching the kid is the only way to respond. Sure, many parents also get so fed up with these bullies that they want to beat the kid, but that is not the way to address anger. So instead, turn your back and walk away. Remind your child that *sticks and stones may break their bones, but words can't do a thing*—unless they allow them in.

The second point to remember is that certain offenses need to be dealt with in particular ways, and when your child is exposed to such behavior, rather follow the formal processes.

### Step 6: Find Healthy Emotional Outlets

While it is essential to identify, acknowledge, and validate your child's feelings, these steps don't bring any emotional relief. The best way to restore your child's inner calm is to find healthy ways to express their emotions.

The following are great examples of such healthy outlets and can be used at any time, but you can also brainstorm with your child to find new and unique ways to get rid of their emotions.

- Doing sports and being active helps to release emotional energy.
- Arts and crafts shifting their focus to a creative project is a wonderful way to calm them down.
- Listen to music.
- Go for a walk.

### Step 7: How About Trying Mindfulness?

Setting the foundation for mindful living at a young age gives your child the edge necessary to set themselves apart. Being mindful means that you are aware of what you see, hear, feel, smell, and taste, as well as any feelings, pain, or discomfort you experience. By teaching your child mindfulness, you are helping them to master self-control which is vital for effective emotional management.

An easy way to teach mindfulness is to take a walk in nature and name the things you see, hear, or smell. Another is to stretch with them, and they can tell you which muscles they feel in their bodies or have their favorite snack while they state what they smell, what it tastes like, the texture of the snack, and how they feel while eating it.

## ACTIVITIES

It is common for children to express any emotion they feel as anger—you may have noticed that some adults portray similar behavior.

### Anger Management

As anger is the most basic and most often expressed emotion, let's start this journey by making anger management a practical exercise.

### What Is Anger Management for Kids?

A child who hasn't learned appropriate or acceptable ways to express their anger tends to portray destructive behavior. Typically, this would be throwing toys, slamming doors, or breaking things. Are you familiar with such behavior in your home?

It can be quite a headache to address, as seeing your child behave in such an unruly manner is upsetting. But unfortunately for many parents, witnessing such an angry outburst in their children also serves as an emotional trigger for them. Then it can become tough to get all the feelings that surface under control.

This is where anger management plays a vital role in helping your child express their anger in acceptable ways. These techniques are easy enough to learn at a young age but will remain valuable to your child into adulthood.

***How Do I Control My Temper?***

Teach your child that when they are angry, they need to answer the following three questions first before taking any action.

***Why Do I Feel Angry?***

By answering the question, your child is forced to shift their focus beyond the emotion they experience to determine what is causing them to feel this way. It also helps to determine any patterns in their behavior and to define and address triggers of the emotion.

***What Happens When I Feel Angry?***

This step serves as a second step in shifting focus away from the feeling to what are the consequences of feeling this way. It is also a question guiding your child to become familiar with the physical side of anger and preparing them to look for alternative ways to express the emotion. For example, rather than being consumed with burning anger, your child can become aware that they feel hot when angry.

***What Should I Do with My Anger?***

This is the final question and stage in the anger management process. Your child needs to identify how they choose to express their anger in acceptable ways. For example, Danny decided that whenever he was angry, he'd rather go and kick the ball in the garden than slam his door.

### *Bye, Bye Uncomfortable Emotions*

This activity is quite a fun one. Fill a couple of balloons with water. Go into the garden and let your child throw these balloons one by one. Consider the water inside as their emotions and help them visualize how every balloon breaking is getting rid of these uncomfortable emotions.

## Handy Worksheets

### *Building Our Feelings Vocabulary*

Visit this worksheet regularly, preferably daily, and help your child understand what each of these emotions means. Pick an emotion for the day or week and discuss with your child what it means, but also see if you can see other people who might experience that particular emotion.

For example, Claire and her mom picked *worry* as the emotion they are exploring for the week, and at that time, Claire could identify that the main character in her animation was worried as he lost his crown.

Some emotions you can use on the worksheet are:

- bored
- confident
- tired
- vulnerable
- sad
- angry
- shy
- cranky
- jealous
- excited

See how many more feelings you can add to the list.

***Requests vs. Demands***

You can help your child understand that simply changing how they ask for something can increase the odds in their favor of getting it.

On your worksheet, list as many demands as you can, some may be familiar in your home, and others may be entirely new. These all fall into the demands column. Opposite each demand, your child can rephrase the demand to become a request. This then becomes your request column.

The demand may be, "You must buy me this toy!" However, this is not an acceptable way to express your needs and wants. The better way to ask for it would be, "Would you please buy me this toy?"

More ideas of demands are:

- Leave me alone!
- Go away!
- It's my turn!

These can be replaced with requests like:

- Would you mind giving me a bit of alone time?
- Can I be on my own right now?
- Can I play now?

***What I Want to Be***

This worksheet guides your child to what is an acceptable way to behave at home and in public.

Divide your worksheet into two columns. On the one side, list what your child doesn't want to be, and on the second column, list what they want to be.

For example:

- I don't want to be angry; I want to be happy.
- I don't want to cry; I want to smile.
- I don't want to be mean; I want to be friendly.

## Developing Emotions the Healthy Way

During every stage in your child's life, they are experiencing a new phase of emotional development, and you can guide them to do so in a healthy way.

### Babies

#### *Messy Play*

Messy play allows your baby to express themselves by using sand, clay, paint, or water. As your child is so young, it will be a messy venture, and it is best to set up a space outside and dress them in clothes that can be ruined. Let them have free access to the medium you are using and have fun with them.

### Toddlers

#### *Puppet Play*

A toddler's imagination is still free and wild, and anything is possible for them. Therefore, they can get lost in a puppet show, soaking up every word and action of the puppets. Use puppets to tell your toddler about emotions as they often identify easier with this type of doll than with what you tell them as their parent.

### Preschoolers

#### *Mirror, Mirror!*

What do the different emotions look like? Familiarize your child with facial expressions that resemble different emotions through the mirror, mirror game. You and your child should sit facing each other, and you can take turns on who is going to be first to pull faces. The other should copy the expression and state what emotion it is showing. It helps your child identify different emotions in others and become more comfortable with embracing their feelings.

### Elementary Schoolers

#### *Red Light, Green Light!*

This is a fun group game in which one player is the red or green light, and whenever the child calls out *the green light,* players can run toward them, and when they shout *red light,* all should stop immediately. Those who fail to do so fall out, and the last one standing wins.

### Middle Schoolers

#### *There Is an App for That!*

By middle school, your child is most likely comfortable with a smart device, and they also consider it to be a much more useful source of information than your words. Use this mindset to your benefit, as there are so many apps available your child can use to help them to become masters of emotional management. Some of my favorites are *DreamyKid* and *Calm Counter,* while the already very popular *Calm* and *Headspace* also have versions for younger users, *calm Kids* and *Headspace for Kids.*

## In Conclusion

Only once your child is confident in who they are and what they feel that they'll be comfortable in social settings. It is why emotional management is the foundation from which they can advance their social skills.

In this chapter, we've explored the emotional needs of every developmental stage and how to support your child in the best possible manner.

I've also added ideas for games you can play at home, putting the fun back into learning. Now, we are taking the next step and discovering the appropriate ways to talk to people.

## 2

# HOW DO I TALK TO PEOPLE?

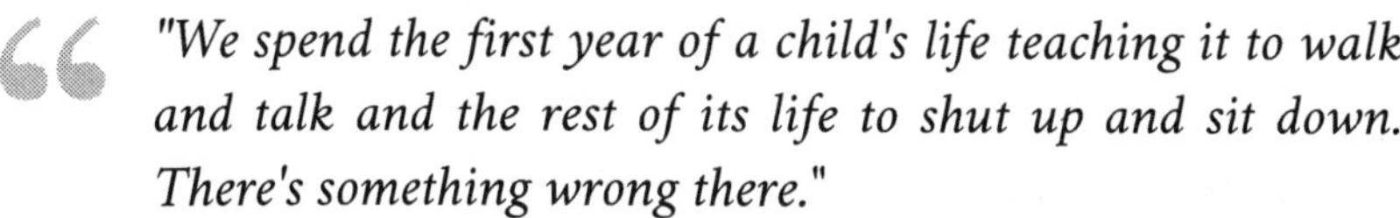

> *"We spend the first year of a child's life teaching it to walk and talk and the rest of its life to shut up and sit down. There's something wrong there."*
>
> — NEIL DEGRASSE-TYSON

The powerful and successful people in life are the ones who are excellent communicators. Even if you are the most intelligent person walking around and you cannot express yourself clearly, getting your audience to understand what you are saying, nobody will ever know what you are capable of. So, the sooner you can help your child communicate clearly, the better it will be for them.

### Communication: What Is It All About?

So often, we take our ability to speak and hear for granted. However, effective communication is necessary to live a life of joy and satisfaction. It is a way to communicate your needs and wants, express your emotions, and connect to others. This is as valid for you as the parent as it is for your child. I've often had parents and kids in my office who are both at their wits' end due to the child's frustration caused by their inability to express their feelings.

**Communication Milestones**

Before we go into any greater detail about how to establish excellent communication skills in your child, we need to look at the different communication milestones for every stage of development until your child turns five. Why five? Well, by the time your little one turns five, their level of speech has developed to the point where they are understandable, and from here onwards, they only expand their vocabulary and develop their speaking style.

- **0-5 Months:** Your baby uses sounds to express themselves. These are in the form of coos, giggles, crying, or fussing noises.
- **6-11 Months:** It is usually during this stage that your baby says their first word. Otherwise, their speech has now expanded to ma-ma, da-da, no-no, and ba-ba, and you'll find that they try to repeat your words.
- **12-17 Months:** They are still trying to repeat simple words, can identify specific words, and may be familiar with about four to six words. Their pronunciation is often still unclear, and they only grasp short words consisting of about four to six letters.
- **18-23 Months:** Now your little one has about 50 words in their vocabulary, even though they still struggle to state them clearly. They can mimic animal sounds and are familiar with mine and what it means. By now, they are also likely to use two-word phrases.

- **2-3 Years:** Their familiarity with spatial concepts, pronouns, and descriptive words has grown substantially. Your child will answer simple questions, and their pronunciation will improve.
- **3-4 Years:** They can identify colors, various objects, clothes, and food. Some sounds are still distorted, but their speech has improved vastly. They can even express their ideas and what they want, and they'll repeat sentences.
- **4-5 Years:** Their spatial expression becomes more advanced, and they know what terms like behind and inside mean. They may still struggle to express certain difficult words, but their answering ability has improved to the where they can answer why questions now. Your child will also start to use past tense verbs.
- **5 Years:** Your child can engage in conversation, describe objects, understand rhyming, and can use sentences of eight words. They share their imaginative stories and use complex sentences.

Are these the norms for all children? No! Never would I want any parent to feel that if their child is not on track with the above timeline, they are falling behind. There are many factors impacting the speed of your child's development. So, if your little one is not yet there, help them along without any pressure.

How can you help your child to improve their communication skills? Let's see.

### Babies (0-1 Year)

Your baby can still only communicate through the most basic sounds and gestures, and yet, you have to start now to help them form a solid foundation to expand on their communication skills.

**Step 1: Always Respond**

Just imagine how frustrating it must be when you are experiencing discomfort and aren't able to ask for the help you need. While babies don't know that they don't know how to talk, they still try their best to communicate that they are hungry, need burping, feel niggly, or even have painful gums to relieve their situation.

It must be severely frustrating not to get the help you seek from mommy, daddy, or whoever is looking after your well-being. Therefore, always respond when your baby needs you. Doing so gives them the security that you'll always be there for them. You may spark emotions like feeling left out or even being rejected by simply ignoring your child.

**Step 2: Be the Tone Model**

Soon, your baby will start to repeat the sounds they hear to make up words. Yet, they don't only copy the sounds but also absorb the tone you are using to express yourself. Babies who grew up amongst a lot of screaming and yelling are inclined to take a similar tone when they are finally ready to express themselves. So, try to stick to a softer tone that is soothing for your baby and all in your home.

**Step 3: NO Screen Time!**

It is very likely that screen time wasn't even a word when you were little. Now, things are completely different, and more and more parents turn to their smart devices to keep their little ones entertained. This is not bad parenting, but much rather desperate parenting as our lives are so pressing to make ends meet that parents have far less time now to spend with their babies than 20 or 30 years ago. However, when we know better, we can do better, and now you know that it is never a good idea to expose your child, who isn't yet two, to screen time. Screen time has no benefits to their development unless your child is included in a video chat.

### Step 4: Always Watch Their Hands

Your child may not be able to express sensible words yet, but they communicate quite a bit through hand movements and gestures. For example, a wave with the hand equates to bye-bye, while they'll make sure you see which way they are pointing when they want something. So be sure to keep your eyes on their hands and see how much they actually speak to you. "For 1-year-olds, using gestures as non-verbal communication is an important skill you can encourage" (Reilly, 2022, para 3).

### Step 5: Use Real Words

The easiest thing is to talk back to your baby using the same sounds they do, and that is fine as long as you mainly stick to using real words. This is because you want their speech to improve to your level, and by giving your little one constant exposure to what real words sound like, they pick up on it much faster.

### Step 6: Play Lots of Games with Sounds

Learning is always easier when it is fun too. Nursery rhymes and songs are an excellent way to help your child learn new sounds and remember them easier as they are part of rhymes. Even a game of peek-a-boo can be squeezed in between as it teaches your baby that they need to wait their turn. See how many of these songs and rhymes you can remember from your childhood days. I bet you'll be surprised that many of these lines are still stuck in your head as you were exposed to them early in life.

### Step 7: Let Them Talk

Listening is as much a part of the communication process as talking. By listening to what your baby is saying, you give them an example of what it means to listen while they feel important too. It doesn't matter that they aren't saying anything you can make sense of, as the most important thing here is to teach them the most basic form of active listening.

## Toddlers (1-3 Years) & Preschoolers (3-5 Years)

Over the years, I've had many concerned parents reaching out to me as all the kids in their child's playgroup are already talking, and theirs are still not there.

### My Toddler Isn't Talking Yet–Should I Be Worried?

The immense pressure parents would experience when their children don't develop as fast as the other kids in the group never cease to amaze me. It is so unnecessary to put yourself under this strain too. I can assure you that many of these parents who once were concerned about their babies not talking yet can get these kids to stop talking at a later stage in life. Every child develops at their own pace, letting them pick up on language skills in their own time.

That said, you can make it easier for them with these steps.

**Step 1: Keep Talking Around Them**

The more you expose your baby to words, the more familiar they'll become with the meaning of the sounds. So, even if you aren't always talking to your baby, keeping the conversation going around is a wonderful way to increase their vocabulary.

**Step 2: But No Baby Talk!**

I've already mentioned that you should limit the baby talk when your baby is still young, and once they become toddlers, especially preschoolers, it is best to avoid this kind of language completely. Of course, you want them to learn as many words as possible to express themselves accurately, but keeping them from using this language at the playschool is also best.

**Step 3: Try the 3 L's**

Look, listen, and learn. When your toddler is excited to share something with you, they easily get overwhelmed and struggle to express themselves. You can help. Let them sit down upright and look you in the eyes or the bridge of your nose—whichever is easiest for them. Listen to what they say and nod when necessary. This will encourage your child to continue with their story. Learn by asking questions and letting them ask you questions. The process of asking and waiting for a reply teaches patience and that you have to wait your turn. It is also a fun way for them to learn new information.

**Step 4: Read Together**

Stories are such fun, and reading time is almost always a time for those precious cuddles. While you two snuggle up for a great story, you expand your child's horizons and expose them to a bunch of new words they can link to the pictures in the book.

**Step 5: Name Items**

When your child is pointing to an object they want, name the object, and let them repeat the word before passing it on to them. Don't wait until after they have it, for then you've lost their focus on the item. For example, if they point to the cup, say *cup* and let them repeat it before handing it to them to explore.

**Step 6: Give Them Choices**

This is especially important for preschoolers. For example, "Do you want to wear a blue or a pink dress?" "Do you want the big cup or the small cup?" Through these choices, your child becomes familiar with the different values attached to words, and it is early exposure to making decisions for themselves.

**Step 7: Expand & Recast**

What does this even mean, right? When your child says something, you can take their sentence and expand on it before giving it back to them. Some examples will make it clearer.

Let's say your little one says, "Red apple." Your reply can be, "Yes, it is a big juicy red apple." Or you can expand a sentence like, "I want grape juice," to "Okay, I'll pour you sweet red grape juice."

**Elementary Schoolers (5-10 Years)**

I've mentioned earlier that once your child turns five, their language skills are usually completely developed. But does that make them eloquent speakers yet? We can only wish. So, until that wish is granted, you can still do a lot to increase your child's vocabulary and help your child develop their unique style of speech.

**Step 1: Active Listening**

Active listening means that you are soaking up every word your child is saying and are not merely present on a physical level while your mind is visiting 1,000 different places. What is even more important is to show your child you are listening, and you can do this by asking questions to learn more about what they are telling you. For example:

- Why did they do it?
- What happened next?
- How did that make you feel?

**Step 2: Reflective Listening**

With this type of listening, you are almost holding up a mirror and reflecting on your child what you've just heard them say. "So, you say there were three biscuits on the plate." Or "So, you were painting flowers in the class today."

**Step 3: "I Don't Know" vs. "I Think"**

Picture this setting. Your child just got home after a long day at school. For the entire day, they were exposed to noisy passages, their classmates causing a racket in the class. They also learned new skills and had to behave well all day long. When they get home, they are tired and don't want to think. When you ask them something simple, they are likely to answer, "I don't know." This statement can be translated as "I don't feel like thinking or answering now." It is also a common escape used by shy kids. Instead of quickly opting out of the conversation, encourage your child to start their sentences with "I think..." This way, they make it clear that they aren't sure whether they are right, but they aren't just putting an end to the possible conversation.

**Step 4: It's Not You–It's What You Did**

Whether you are dealing with an adult or a child, it is always important to refrain from transforming someone's actions into their personality type. For example, just compare the following two sentences:

- You are a liar.
- You are lying.

While the first condemns the personality, the second criticizes the behavior. Therefore, always separate your child from their behavior as you condemn the latter.

**Step 5: How Was Your Day?**

I love taking drives with my kids. The secret is to take only one at a time. Then you eliminate the chance that one child may take over the conversation, and there is nowhere for them to go, so they may just as well talk to you. This is a good time to ask questions like the following:

- How was your day?
- What did you enjoy the most about your day?
- What was really bad?
- What made you mad today?

- Who made you laugh?

**Step 6: Explain Body Language**

Picking up non-verbal cues doesn't just come naturally for all. Some kids struggle to read what emotions their playmates are experiencing, making it hard to respond or reach out effectively. Teach your child from early onwards what body language is and practice it with them.

**Step 7: Learn How to Take Turns**

Life is often about waiting your turn to ensure a smooth flow. Sometimes, you may also need to give up your turn to accommodate another. However, effective communication demands that you wait your turn and that you do so patiently. Whether you want to instill the importance of taking turns through sports or board games or in any other way that fits your family dynamics, keep in mind that this will also help your child improve at communication. The last thing you would want is for them to get a reputation for being rude as they always interrupt their friends, and neither would you want that to be the case at home.

**Middle Schoolers (10+)**

Just like with kids in elementary school, you only need to help your middle schooler to expand their vocabulary to help them become better at expressing themselves. Conversations with your middle schooler are no different from those with an adult friend. It may just be content that varies.

### Step 1: Listen

Not just hearing but actually listening is a skill so many of us need to improve. Unfortunately, our minds are far too often busy compiling our answers when someone—including our children—talks rather than absorbing every bit of shared information. Thus, practicing listening to your middle schooler will improve your listening skills in all other conversations. Furthermore, by doing so, you also set an example for your child to become a better listener. This is a win-win situation.

### Step 2: Acknowledge Feelings

One of the most basic needs we all feel is that we matter to someone else and that our feelings matter. This is exactly the message that comes across when you acknowledge your child's feelings. Essentially, you are telling them that they and their feelings matter to you. That is a special bond to share.

### Step 3: Don't Jump in And Correct Them Immediately

It may be tempting to correct your child when they are wrong immediately. But stop! What message is coming across when you do? Is it the kind of message that will encourage your child to communicate more? Will it instill confidence in them as speakers?

No, none of these will be the result when you interrupt your child. Furthermore, it isn't polite, and you are setting an example that it is acceptable. It is not. Not when you talk to your spouse or coworkers and also not when you talk to your child. Always remember, they are looking at the example you set all the time!

**Step 4: Enjoy Movies & Shows Together**

For the longest time, you've been the one who decides what your child will eat, wear, watch, do, and where they'll go. You've also determined when they'll do all these things. Make a point of doing something fun with your child, which is their choice. Watch a movie with them that they want to see. Take them to a show of their favorite band. Let them choose, as this indicates that their choices and desires count too. How will this improve their communication skills? Giving your child this kind of freedom increases their confidence, and confidence and communication go hand-in-hand.

**Step 5: Establish a Code Word**

Code words are fun as there is a sense of exclusivity linked to it. Only you and your child know what the code word means. You can use these code words to have your child confirm that they are safe, happy, or doing well. But you can also get code words that indicate, "I don't feel like talking right now." Or even "I love you." Believe me, this becomes especially important when they reach the stage where a public declaration of their love for mom or dad has vanished.

**Step 6: Ask for Their Opinion**

This is another confidence booster. Who doesn't like to know that their opinion matters, right? By reaching out to your child for their opinion, you are setting an example and a trend that they can reach out to you in the same manner. You also tell them what they think is important to you.

### Step 7: Eat Together

Maybe your lives are so busy that having the traditional family dinner every night is impossible. It is okay if you can't make it so often; make sure that it becomes a family tradition to have at least certain nights of the week dinner as a family. You can set the rules for this tradition and try to make sure everyone attends. These dinners are a great time to bond and encourage group conversation.

## ACTIVITIES

Pushing your child to talk more than they are comfortable doing is not a good idea. Just think how you'll feel if you are forced to do something uncomfortable. You'll be inclined to do just the opposite if we are in any way alike. That said, there are many things you can do to help them get more comfortable talking to others so that they'll interact more often out of their free will. This is true for every stage of their lives. The following activities will improve your child's communication.

### Babies

During this stage, you want your baby to become more familiar with certain words and connect the word's meaning to the sound you are making.

#### *Name the Body Part*

This game is a fun interaction between you and your child to achieve the above outcome. When your baby is in a good mood, spend time with them and point and touch every part of their body, naming it out loud. A tickle on the belly while saying *tummy* or touching their toes while saying *toe* is all you need to do right now.

## Toddlers

It is best to get your silly on to effectively interact with your toddler.

### *Copycat, That!*

This is a game for one-on-one play. First, you can mimic an animal, and then it is your child's turn to copy that. Next, it is your child's turn; you must copycat that. Throughout the play, you can use words like *my turn, your turn,* or make the sounds of the animal you mimic. The most important rule is to have fun, though.

## Preschoolers

By now, your child has had their first exposure to taking turns and how important it is to wait your turn. Yet, it is a lesson you'll continuously have to reinforce.

### *Taking Turns*

This game works well if you have another child to play with. Under your supervision, you can make sure that they take turns playing with special toys, but you can also up the challenge a little.

Give each child 30 seconds to name all the objects with wheels or faces they can see in the room. When one child is naming these things, the other may not interrupt. Once the time has passed, the other kids must say a few things about the one whose turn it was mentioned.

## Elementary Schoolers

For many kids across the globe, like in the States, their social status in elementary school becomes the foundation of where they fit in for the rest of their school years. Therefore, it is normal to want your child to feel like they fit in during this time in their lives. Great communication skills and knowing how to talk, listen, and read body language will surely help them in this quest.

### *Back-to-Back*

Do you have a couple of tweens in your care? Line them up and let them sit back-to-back in pairs. One kid must have paper and a pen to draw the picture the other one is describing. Using a completely nonsensical picture is best, as this will make it harder and more fun. Once they are done, compare the images to see who did the best in communicating what they saw and listened to what their partner said.

### *What are They Feeling?*

Have fun and treat yourself and your child to a milkshake, and while you sip on your well-deserved treats, play a game, "What are They Feeling?" Look at the people around you and try to figure out what everyone's body language is stating. It is a way to practice body language observation with your child.

## Middle Schoolers

Are you ready for more advanced games?

### *Back-to-Back Scattergories*

Each kid in the group must have a piece of paper with every letter of the alphabet on it, and next to it, there must be a space for a word. They'll have a limited time, and in this time, they must write down a word for every letter of the alphabet that is linked to school, sports, or any other fun topic you can think about. For example, if you use sports, then *A* can stand for *athlete*. The idea is to use words you think others may not have on their list, as you only score a point when nobody else has the word.

***Continuous Stories***

You can play this game as a family or when your kids have a group of friends over. One person starts a story, and someone else must pick up on it and continue when they stop. Every child needs to get a turn. These stories can take the craziest turns, but that is all part of the fun while it encourages group communication. You can limit the game, allowing every child to only say one sentence before it is the turn of the next one.

## In Conclusion

From the moment your child is born, they have reasons to communicate, express themselves, and ask for what they need. Then, their ability to do so accurately improves as they grow older.

By the time your child turns five, the foundation for communication has been laid, and now you only need to encourage them to express themselves and help them expand their vocabulary.

Rather than stressing about your child not meeting the set milestones, help them with fun games. Remember that the emphasis is always on *fun*, as it makes learning a much better and more effective experience.

# 3

# HOW DO I MAKE FRIENDS?

*"The only way to have a friend is to be one."*

— RALPH WALDO EMERSON

Friendship is a two-way street. The sooner you can teach—and demonstrate—that to your kids, the happier they'll be in their friendships throughout their lives. The worst kind of friend is one that only expects others to be there for them but seldom, if ever, shows up when you need them. Like me, you, too, most likely had a point in your life where you had to address a one-sided friendship that became just so draining it had no future prospects. Furthermore, I firmly believe that we need to raise our kids to grow into adults we want to be friends with one day. Yes, your babies may still be so tiny and dependent, but this will pass. It is such a beautiful thing to watch elderly parents with their adult children when you can see that, except for the parental bond, they are really great friends too. So, whatever seeds you sow now will bear fruits for many years to come.

## You're Never too Young for Friends

We've all had friends that came and went in our lives. They are there merely for a season. Then those special people remain part of our lives through every phase and stage. So, yes, for sure, contact might be more or less at times, but the connection remains intact.

Friendship is far more than merely a way to pass your time. Friends play an essential role in the development of the human brain; therefore, your child is never too young to have friends. Through various friendships, children see themselves through their peers' eyes. These bonds confirm to them that they are accepted by their own, and every new friendship is a practice run to forming such a vital connection. Friendships and the bond between peers also allow you to reinvent yourself until you feel comfortable in your identity. Not to even mention how we rely on our friends for support, understanding, and stress relief. While family bonds are vital connections, your friendships may become even more precious ones to cherish.

So, are you ready to see how you can help your little ones prepare to have meaningful friendships from an early age?

## Babies (0-1 Year) & Toddlers (1-3 Years)

It is never too early to encourage your baby to make friends. Yes, even when they are still so young, and all they do is lie on the same playmat, cooing at each other at intervals, a social connection is forming that sets the foundation for many friendships over the years.

### Step 1: Small & Short Playdates

Playdates can take place in a setting that is familiar to your child, like at your home, in a new and unfamiliar location, like a friend's home, or even in a neutral space, like a park. In each of these settings, your child will be exposed to a new learning experience; therefore, having these playdates is good. But as your child is still very young, it is best to keep the group of friends limited to only a few and to keep them short.

### Step 2: Look, There's Another Person–Smile!

Has it ever happened to you that you are busy with grocery shopping or any other mundane task, and suddenly you make eye contact with a stranger, smile at them and get nothing in return? Doesn't this immediately trigger your defense response? I mean, how hard is it to smile back at someone, right?

Smiling at them is the most basic indication to show that you are interested and open to getting to know a stranger better. Therefore, it helps to instill this idea early on in your child by practicing identifying other people and immediately smiling when you make contact. Make smiling part of their natural response to seeing others and help them connect easily.

### Step 3: Set an Example

I've said it before, and I'll say it many more times, not because it is anything you didn't know but because we can so easily forget that there are precious eyes on us the entire time. So, if you want your children to be great friends to their friends and grow into socially accepted people, then you need to be all those things first to model the typical behavior to them. Then, you set the example, and they'll follow your lead.

**Step 4: Take Things Slow**

Meeting too many people can be overwhelming and even scare your child off making friends for a bit. Also, your child may still be way too young to determine whether they are introverted or extroverted. For example, imagine you have a little introvert in your home, and then you overwhelm them with many friends at once. This can easily turn into a rather bad experience for them. So instead, stick to small groups and meet only one or two friends at a time.

**Step 5: Play Lots of Pretend!**

If you are like me, you, too, prefer to have some idea of what a situation is going to be like before stepping into it. Yet, children of this age can be highly unpredictable, and a fun event can quickly turn into an embarrassing discomfort. But you can prepare your child for what will happen and, in this way, guide them on how to react and behave when meeting new or familiar friends. Do this by playing pretend, and once the date arrives, you both have an idea of what the possible challenges are going to be and how you can handle them gracefully.

**Step 6: Read Them Books About Friendship**

There are so many books available about friendships and how to be great friends. Some of the old classics which I love are *The Wizard of Oz* and, of course, anything *Winnie the Pooh* related, but there is also much never literature you can share with your child.

The more you read these stories to them, the more they become familiar with the characters and are open to learning from them.

**Step 7: How About a Pet?**

Don't underestimate the friendship bond that can form between a child and a pet. Pets are so loyal and fun too. Added is the fact that pets require some level of responsibility from your child, providing them with an example of how to be a great friend first.

**Preschoolers (3-5 Years)**

Your child is not at the age where you can see they are having fun with other kids their age. This is often the time in your life that includes many playdates and attending numerous birthday parties. Yet, if it is not the case for you and your child, taking the following steps will surely help to ease the topic of friendship in your home.

**Step 1: Note Potential Candidates**

Do you know who your child prefers to play with in the park or at daycare? What names come up regularly when they share their day with you? Once you've identified a good match or two for your child, invite them for a playdate to give your child a chance to strengthen their friendship.

**Step 2: Practice Saying Hello!**

This is another instance where you'll have to model the behavior first before you can encourage your child to do the same. When you meet a stranger, say hello and ask their name. Encourage your child to do the same when they see a child they've never met.

Saying hello and introducing yourself can also take on the form of a fun pretend session.

**Step 3: Playdates! My Place or Yours?**

If your child is somewhat shy, they may feel more at ease hosting a playdate than attending one in an unfamiliar setting. However, it may also be that the child you want your little one to befriend is the shy one, and then it is best to be open to an invitation to their home.

**Step 4: Be Open About Values in Friendship**

Your preschooler is not yet advanced enough to converse deeply about values. Heck, they'll not have the faintest idea of what you are talking about if you mention values to them. But they understand what it means to be nice to their friends, friendly to new mates at school, and helpful. So express your values to your child in a manner they understand and encourage them to make friends who behave in these ways too.

**Step 5: Encourage Socializing**

Encourage your child to make friends. Tell—and show—them how important your friends are to you and that having friends is a good thing. Try to refrain from ever criticizing their friends or expressing that attending their parties and playdates is a burden to you.

**Step 6: "You're Not My Friend!" – Uh-Oh!**

Already at this stage, children are forming groups of friends, and it is to be expected that at some point, your child may want to join such a group and be excluded from it. Or it may be that they have to meet certain criteria before getting included; for example, they may have to invite a specific kid to a party to "gain" their friendship.

This is as much of a painful experience at their age as at any other age, and all you can do is be there for them. Offer comfort and encouragement that better friends are waiting for them to be found.

**Step 7: Stay Close!**

Don't let kids play unsupervised. You don't have to hover over them the entire time but stay close. These kids are all still in different stages of development, and it is better to defuse a heated situation as soon as you notice something is happening than to clean up the mess afterward. Also, if your child didn't have fun at another kid's home, you will not likely agree to another playdate, and other parents will react similarly. So, rather ensure a peaceful and pleasant playdate than have to take care of the social implications later on.

### Elementary Schoolers (5-10 Years)

At this stage, making friends can be challenging for the socially poorly equipped kid. If this is your kid, it can be heartbreaking to witness. However, the following steps will surely ease the situation.

**Step 1: Prep Time**

There is nothing wrong with preparing your child for this interaction. Do you have a playdate coming up? Chat with your child about the fun time before it takes place. Get some ideas of fun things they can do or what they can do to get things going. Parents often mention, and I saw in my kids, too, that they would have a friend over, and for the first half—if not more—of the scheduled time, they would be like strangers to each other. Then when they finally get to play together nicely, playtime is over too soon for their liking. So, prepare your child to make that connection sooner or even on how to react if the playdate is declined.

### Step 2: Friends Come in All Shapes & Sizes

Not all their friends need to be the same. Encourage your child to allow for diversity in their social circle. It is how they'll learn from early on that it is okay to be different and that each friend can fulfill a different role in their lives. For example, some friends are best to talk to, while others like to be active and run around more. Help them understand that every friend is valuable and should be appreciated for their unique contribution. On a side note, avoid inviting friends that are vastly different all at once. Doing so can put these kids and your child in an uncomfortable position.

### Step 3: Get to Know Your Kid's Friends

By getting familiar with your kid's friends, you get to know their parents, does their family have similar values as yours, what influence these kids will have on your child, and what they are like in general. In addition, it will give you the information you need to encourage some friendships and discourage others.

### Step 4: Keep Those Emotions Regulated

Remember how we spoke about emotions in the first chapter? Now is the time to bring these lessons into practice. Emotionally out-of-control children find it much harder to make and keep friends. If you notice this concern, it is time for a refresher to see how you can support your child to become better at emotional management.

**Step 5: Avoid Comparing!**

Sure, your firstborn is a social butterfly, and your second is a hermit. It doesn't mean that you've failed your second child or something is wrong with them. No, they are just differently wired when it comes to being social. Instead of criticizing or comparing one to the other, encourage both in their unique ways.

**Step 6: Practice, Practice, Practice**

You can still do it at this stage, just like you've had to practice for a playdate when your child was younger. However, when your child is familiar with the setting as you've practiced a playdate—possibly through roleplay—they'll be more confident in their ability to be social. This can be especially helpful if your child is very shy.

**Step 7: Remember, Your Child Still Needs You!**

If your child isn't a baby anymore, they are still not socially mature enough to know what type of friend they want to be or to have. They may need help approaching new friends correctly or successfully handling friction in an existing friendship. They still need you to advise and guide them along the way.

**Middle Schoolers (10+)**

This is the time when your child's social status can be made or broken. Unfortunately, it also appears to be a time when the true drama of childhood friendships becomes complicated. Therefore, even if your kids feel old enough to care for themselves, they still need your guidance.

**Step 1: Refresh Social Cues**

Some kids struggle to read or interpret social cues. They may also send out the wrong signals and suffer severe embarrassment caused by social blunders. Watch your child when they interact socially and see if there is anything in their demeanor needing to be addressed. For example, your child struggles to respect personal space. Or they don't pick up on tone or mannerisms when others talk, guide them without being criticized. You can even use examples of people doing it right and those who are getting it all wrong.

**Step 2: Remind Your Child: Friends Come in Different Shapes & Sizes!**

Social pressure may rise, and your child may feel increased strain to break off friendships with dear but weird friends who don't enjoy the approval of the social crowd your child is part of. Recap on the talk that friends come in all shapes and sizes, and dropping a friend for being different is not cool. Ask them how they'd feel if someone doesn't want to be friends anymore, as they are considered weird.

**Step 3: What Is a Good Friend?**

A good friend is available when you need them, respects you, can be trusted, can give and receive compliments easily, understand your feelings, and can disagree without hurting your feelings. Focus on the features you want to see in your child's friends rather than focusing on the attributes of people you don't want them to befriend.

**Step 4: Work on Their Listening Skills**

We've spoken about this before too. Good friends listen to each other. Is your child a good listener? Do their friends listen to them? If not, it is time to remind your child of the importance of listening and to surround yourself with people willing to listen to you.

**Step 5: Consider After-School Activities & Other Avenues**

Most friends your child will make at school, but if they struggle to make good friends here, encourage them to take up activities or hobbies they enjoy and join a club or an after-school activity. They'll be exposed to many kids with similar interests here, and making friends will be much easier.

**Step 6: Positively Reinforce Good Friendship Traits**

Consistently remind your child what it means to be a good friend. Then, live by your example and applaud them for being great friends by showing these traits and encourage them to respect themselves enough not to tolerate friendships that don't portray these traits.

**Step 7: Boundaries Are Very Important**

Before your child respects the boundaries of others, they would have to start to value theirs first. So, again, your example in this regard will carry the most weight, but also explain to your child how important it is to set and protect boundaries, and they need to consider the boundaries of others, too, to be great friends.

## ACTIVITIES

### *Friendship Stoplight Game*

This is a wonderful activity for preschoolers, those in elementary school, and even younger middle schoolers.

Cut out three cardboard circles and color them so you have a red, yellow, and green circles. Attach them to a board or wall in the same format as a stoplight. The red circle symbolizes features you don't want in friends or friendships. The yellow indicates acceptable attributes, and the green is the characteristics you want to see in a friendship or your friends. Then you can share different scenarios with the kids or read cards with statements about friendship like "Sally never wants to give anyone a turn." The kids must then decide whether this belongs to the red, yellow, or green light. This game leans itself to be open to as much discussion as you like.

### Let's Make Friends!

### Babies

### *Let's Read*

You are still very limited in what you can do to help your baby to make friends, but one of the steps you can follow is to read to them about friendships.

Even though they may not understand everything you read, something will find a place in their minds, and then there are also the many other benefits you and your little one will enjoy from reading. There are so many fun books to choose from; these books usually have the most amazing pictures to captivate their attention.

## Toddlers

### *Color Block Match*

Now you'll be able to do quite a bit more with your little one, and the following game is a great way to help them to become comfortable with breaking the ice and making new friends.

This game can be played when you have a group of toddlers who are all new to each other. Give each child a large building block, and they must walk around the room to find everyone with the same color block. When they do, they have to introduce themselves to each other.

## Preschoolers

### *Show and Tell*

Your child is now old enough to share some information about themselves with the group. This activity is a way to practice introducing yourself to a larger group of kids.

Every kid should bring something they treasure from home. It can be a favorite toy or blanket, coloring book, or even their favorite snack. Then, every kid in the group will get a turn to show what they've brought and tell the others what it is and why it is so important.

## Elementary Schoolers

### *Telephone Game*

I still remember how much fun and laughter this game brought to my elementary school years. Later on, it became something we would play with the kids in the family, too, when all the cousins got together.

The kids need to sit in a line, and then you'll whisper a secret message or even a one-liner into the ear of the first child. After that, they must continue along the line, whispering what they've heard to the child next to them so they work down the line. The last child then needs to say what they've heard. Usually, this is when the group explodes with laughter, as this message vastly differs from what they've heard and what was initially said.

## Middle Schoolers

### *Lined-Up Commons*

Kids of this age group may be less inclined to play games than when they were much younger. Yet, they still need help to make friends and be sociable, and the next game can help to achieve this.

If the group is too big, divide it into groups of about five or six kids. The purpose of the game is to see how much every child has in common with the others, even though they may appear vastly different. As this is a game of speed, added excitement is linked to getting it right first.

Ask the kids to line up in order of their age, with the youngest in front and the oldest at the back. They can also line up in alphabetical order, height, and hair color, with blonde in front, black at the back, or even hair length. There is no limit to how many times you want these kids to line up, and the group who did this the fastest and could organize themselves in the correct order are the winners.

## In Conclusion

Remember to consider how important friends are in your child's life. Even from as little as being a mere baby, being in the presence of peers impacts their mental, physical, emotional, and social wellness.

Just like us adults, not all children are equally sociable. Even in families, you may find one child to be a social butterfly, and the other may prefer to remain in the cocoon. Don't compare them, and don't judge them, either. Instead, guide them to find friends who may be diverse but share similar values.

Teach them, but even more importantly, show them that to have great friends, you need to be one too. And never settle for anyone who doesn't appreciate your friendship. Rather deal with the painful emotions on your terms than the heartache when you are tagged in a crowd that doesn't care.

# 4

# HOW DO I COMFORT MY FRIENDS?

*"If you see someone without a smile, give them one of yours."*

— DOLLY PARTON

Can you even imagine a world without empathy? Without understanding the joy and heartache, the hardships and the happy moments of celebration of another? Living in such a place sounds very dreary to me. It will keep us from connecting with each other on a deeper level.

## Why Empathy Matters

We can divide empathy into two categories. First, there is a type of empathy that allows us to feel the pain of another without experiencing it ourselves called *emotional empathy*. And then there is our ability to look at people and recognize their emotions by looking at their facial expressions, body language, and gestures, called

### Step 1: Use "I" Messages

"I don't like it when you bite me. It hurts Mommy."

A simple sentence like this, coupled with a suitable facial expression when your little one hurts you, tells them that you condone their behavior but not them. It also teaches them that their actions hurt someone else and that they must be more careful about how they treat others.

This may appear so insignificant that it may not even be worth your effort, but trust me, it is. It is how you set the foundation for future communication and provide even your tiny baby with the understanding that certain types of behavior are good and others are not.

### Step 2: Model Empathy

Remember that your kids learn far more from watching you than listening to what you tell them, especially at this age. If you want your child to be empathetic, you must show them empathy. Comfort and cuddle them when they are upset or hurt. Laugh with them when they are cooing happily. Even when they did something wrong, and you are reprimanding them, your behavior can still portray empathy, dismissing the idea that only certain times or circumstances allow for empathy to be present.

### Step 3: Stay Upbeat and Reassuring

You may not even notice it, but your baby, as young as seven months old, is observing your every action. They learn from your behavior and how you treat others. For example, if you welcome people into your home, they'll consider that person a friend. On the other hand, if you seem upset when you drop them off at daycare, they'll make a negative link to the place and will most likely cry too. Through this observation, they learn, and they copy you. So, opt for the upbeat version of yourself as your little one finds that to be much more reassuring.

**Step 4: Validate–Even at Their Young Age!**

Comforting a sick baby and telling them that you know they feel bad but that Mommy will soon make them feel better is a perfect confirmation of your empathy for what they are going through. Or when your baby is niggly because they've missed nap time, reassuring them you know they don't feel good fulfills the same purpose. Your baby may not grasp the meaning of your words, but your tone and body language express comfort and understanding and model empathy behavior.

**Step 5: Point Out Rude Behavior**

Was your kid acting out? Maybe downright rude to a sibling, parent, or even a grandparent? Highlight their unacceptable behavior and make it clear that such behavior won't be tolerated. Always take care to criticize the behavior and not the child.

**Step 6: Be Kind–Especially When Baby's Watching**

Take note of the moments when your child is watching you and give them an outstanding display of empathy. Then, as they observe your every move, you may make the most of the moments you are on stage.

**Step 7: Be Patient!**

Yes, your child has been born with the inherent ability to show empathy, but you still need to invest the time and effort to help them develop this part of their personality. It is time-consuming without instant gratification, and you need to remain patient.

**Toddlers (1-3 Years) & Preschoolers (3-5 Years)**

While your child can now observe and express empathy much more effectively than a year or two years ago, they still need to be the poster child for empathy. But, nope, you still find yourself too often bringing calm after the emotional storm their immense lack of empathy brings to your home.

**Step 1: Don't Force an Apology**

Managing the lack of empathy in one child can be challenging. Still, if you are a parent of two or even more toddlers or preschoolers, you may find yourself so frustrated that you simply want to force an apology out of the guilty party and move on with your day. Don't.

By doing so, you may get the response you're looking for—an apology—for sure but don't consider this as an achievement. All that happened is you've asked your little ones to do something they're not developed to do yet. They are still becoming familiar with their own emotions and don't consider the feelings of another yet. So, they don't understand why they apologize and can see Mommy or Daddy is angry, so they'll likely feel shame for making this mistake.

**Step 2: Be the Model**

As your child is still becoming familiar with their emotions, the most important thing you can do for them right now is to stick with being an exceptional role model for them.

**Step 3: Look for Teaching Opportunities**

Maintain a constant awareness of possible teachable moments to come along during the day. I believe that practical life situations make for the best learning opportunities. Chat to your kid about their day, and be alert when they mention friends or even their teacher and ask them what they think they feel. For example, "How do you think your friend felt when his ice cream fell on the floor?" or "What do you think your teacher felt like when you gave her flowers this morning?" These and similar questions pique their interest in thinking about the emotions of another.

**Step 4: Let Them Hear "I'm Sorry"**

The phrase "I'm sorry" is sometimes a double-edged sword. Yes, you want to hear your child say they are sorry, but how often do they hear you say the same? Again, model the behavior you want them to follow.

If you are going to force your child to say that they are sorry and they don't understand what they are sorry for, it truly has no meaning. Before getting a sorry, you need to guide their focus to realize that what they did makes someone else feel sad. Then, you have to ask them what they think the other person feels.

**Step 5: Normalize Sharing and Discussing Feelings**

This one is really easy. The more you encourage your family to discuss your feelings and make emotions a common talking point in your home, the greater your kid's familiarity with emotions will become. Thus, the more in tune they'll grow with what they feel and see in others.

**Step 6: Emphasize the Importance of Being Polite**

Sometimes, there is a very fine line between being polite and empathetic. For example, if your child is going to demand something and isn't very polite, they will most likely not get what they want because they make the other person feel bad or angry. But on the other hand, if they are polite and ask nicely, using words like please and thank you, they make the other person feel good and will likely get what they want.

**Step 7: Always Validate Their Feelings**

Children mostly mirror the behavior they observe at home and on the playground. So if you dismiss their feelings at home, they'll do the same to their friends at school. But if you validate what they feel at home and leave them assured that it is okay to feel that way, then that is what they'll mirror toward their friends when you aren't around.

**Elementary Schoolers (5-10 Years)**

This is often the stage in your child's life when you can notice a rapid increase in awareness of what others feel. The following scene will always remind me of the caring nature of kids this age. I was fetching one of my kids from school, and as I was waiting, I noticed a girl fall. Her one knee got scraped and was bleeding a little. The tears were rolling down her cheeks from the moment she came back up. Almost instantly, five girls similar to her age—I guessed about seven years old—came to her rescue and swarmed around her, comforting her, and took her by the hand while another carried her bag. Children in this age group can be highly aware of what others feel. Therefore, your guidance in this regard may have to change its approach slightly.

**Step 1: Talk About Sensations**

It is time to create a greater awareness of the physical sensations that emotions cause in the body. Ask them how they physically feel when they are sad, happy, angry, excited, or upset. If you see someone crying, ask your child what they think that person is feeling or what it was like for them when they felt like that.

**Step 2: Provide Opportunities for Empathy**

Often, parents regret missing out on opportunities to teach their kids empathy as they're at school while the parents are at work. Don't worry, it's fine. You can create occasions demanding empathy. For example, have family meetings to discuss what everyone is feeling. During these meetings, all must listen to what other family members say and try to understand their feelings. Then, they can also expect others to listen when they are talking. Or you can chat with them about their day. For example, ask how they've helped a friend in need or what they can do the next day to make someone's day better.

### Step 3: Look at the Face

To be empathic demands that you are observant of facial expressions, can read them correctly, and know what emotions they indicate. The best way to get your child familiar with all of this is to mimic facial expressions so that recognizing emotions becomes easier for them.

### Step 4: "How Do You Think They Feel?"

By this stage, your child grasps what "cause and effect" is—as we've discussed earlier on. Now you can support the growth of greater awareness by asking them how they think their actions or words made another feel.

### Step 5: Model What Healthy Resolution Looks Like

Yes, you can be sure by now that this step will be listed once again. You are still the best role model, and how you express empathy will rub off on them. Instead, show your child what you expect rather than tell them what they need to do.

### Step 6: Use Activities to Introduce & Nurture Perspective

Learning made fun is effective learning. Therefore, always find fun activities to help your child become more familiar with empathy and comfortable showing it. At the end of the chapter, I am sharing several fun activities in this regard.

### Step 7: Praise Empathetic Behavior

I am sure you have heard the saying that *you catch more flies with honey than vinegar*. It may even be that it is a line you often use to reprimand your kids when they are nasty to others. Now, you should apply this rule too. You'll achieve greater success with developing empathy in your child by complimenting them every time they are getting it right than by pointing out every time they've failed. So, keep on praising positive behavior and see the difference in your child.

**Middle Schoolers (10+)**

The extent of social pressure on children in this age group is frightening. However, today, our kids find themselves in situations that demand to show more empathy and are present for their friends rather than turning toward the—sometimes extremely harsh—social opinion of their peers. Regardless of what the contributing factors are to this, it is important to help your child to become better at showing empathy and to be supportive friends.

**Step 1: CARE**

CARE is an acronym that will help you guide your kids to care more for their friends. The following steps will help you to address the lack of empathy in your child's behavior:

- **C**all their attention to their behavior, showing a lack of care.
- **A**ssess how their actions or words impacted others to help them better understand what it means to step into someone else's shoes.
- **R**epair the hurt. Help your child plan a solution for apologizing for the hurt they've caused and repairing the relationship.

- Express your disappointment. You need to make your child aware that such behavior won't be tolerated, as it is hurtful. Also, make it clear what type of behavior you would expect from them in the future.

**Step 2: Watch Their Social Media Use**

Behaving without empathy in a face-to-face situation may still be prevented by the pressure of social norms. Still, social media platforms create an opportunity to behave easily in such a manner without facing any consequences for your words or actions. Adults are guilty of this type of behavior, and even more so for kids who fall into this age group. Monitor your child's social media use and encourage your children to follow a balanced approach toward the amount of time they spend on these platforms.

**Step 3: Polish Face-Reading Skills**

As empathy depends mainly on your ability to correctly read the expressions of others to determine their emotional state, you can continuously work on your child's ability to read the expressions of others. For example, look at people or photos and let your child tell you what they think the other person is feeling.

**Step 4: Keep Practicing What You Preach**

When kids are young, they watch your every move to learn from you as they model your behavior. As they grow older, especially from this age group onwards into their teenage years, children watch your behavior and keep track of your every move to remind them of where you went wrong in your actions. It means that the older children become, the more you need to consider your behavior and remember that your actions are constantly being watched. I know it sucks, right? After all, parents are human too, but that is just the reality of life, and there is not much we can do to change it.

**Step 5: Help Them Manage Their Feelings**

In the first chapter, we discussed how important it is to manage your feelings to sustain friendships. This lesson needs to be highlighted once more when it comes to empathy. It is only possible to truly show empathy toward another if your feelings are under control. Therefore, regularly check in with your child to help them manage their feelings well.

**Step 6: Cultivate a Moral Identity**

Being an empathetic adult requires more than just always doing the right thing. It would be best if you also wanted to do the right thing, as that is how your moral identity guides you through life. Yes, sure, while your kids were still very young, it was enough to praise them when they did well and to address their behavior when they didn't. However, now they are older; you have to support your child to cultivate their moral identity, meaning they have to see themselves as caring people to whom the feelings and thoughts of others matter.

## ACTIVITIES

While all kids are born with the ability to be empathetic, it remains a complex concept for some to understand and develop. But you can help your child to master this skill, a skill playing a vital role in the fabric of society. These activities will help you to guide your kids to become more empathetic.

## Babies, Toddlers & Preschoolers

A fun, sing-along way of teaching.

***Yankee Doodle Feelings Song***

Are you familiar with the tune of *Yankee Doodle*? If not, you can, of course, use the tune of any other song that is easy to learn and simply change the words to bring across the message of how important it is to notice and care for the feelings of others.

While singing these songs, you can use exaggerated gestures to help bring the message across. For example, the following snippet is sung to the tune of *Yankee Doodle* (Fitzgerald, 2022 para 17).

The expression on my face (Point a finger around your face).

It is like an open book (Place your hands like a book).

You can read how I am feeling (Put your hand to your heart).

Given how my face looks (Point a finger around your face).

## Elementary & Middle Schoolers: Perspective Taking

***Nice Things***

Surround yourself with positive people and shift your mind to focusing on the good things in your life. These two action steps are the foundation that makes it possible to lift your mood with little effort, which is exactly what you'll achieve through this exercise.

This game is best played in a classroom or even when you have many kids over for a playdate. Ask the kids in the group to each share something nice they have or have done to the child sitting next to them.

Once the entire class is done, they can share it with the whole class or even get the child they've shared their story to share it with the class on their behalf. The exercise quickly ripples out into multiplying positive emotions that lift the group's mood for the whole day. It also allows the group to feel that they've shared something personal and that what is important to them matters to the group too.

***Thank You, Post***

Only some people are as comfortable speaking up in front of a crowd, and the following exercise may do the trick for those who are shyer and more hesitant to state their feelings.

While this is a great game to play in a classroom, you can also use it as a fun learning experience when you have many kids over at your home or even when you are in charge of entertaining kids on a camp. All the kids need to write thank you notes. They can share anything they are grateful for or even letters to encourage a friend. Have a thank you post box where these messages can be posted and read either daily or weekly.

***Emotions Charade***

Who doesn't like charades? I mean, really, it is such a fun activity whether you play it as a family or have a group of friends together. It is a game to be played by young and old.

One kid can portray a specific emotion to play emotion charades, and the group needs to guess which emotion it is. This way, the game makes it fun to spot and identify the emotions we all experience at times.

You can write several emotions on paper slips, and whoever's turn it is to do the charade, draw a paper, and have to express the feeling. When you have a younger crowd, it is best to use simpler emotions like anger, surprise, sadness, happiness, or excitement. You can also include worry, boredom, embarrassment, frustration, and confusion for older kids.

## Middle Schoolers

### *Roleplay*

In this age group, it is essential to help children to understand what it means to look at things from someone else's perspective and to determine what emotions these people are likely experiencing. You can use any character from a lesson plan, prescribed reading, or even history for the following exercise. First, the kids need to pick a person they would like to be and write a paragraph about that person in a specific event. Then, they need to focus on what that person is feeling, what is driving them to do or say certain things, and how these actions influence the lives of others around them.

### *"I Feel" vs. "You Feel"*

Empathy demands you go beyond your feelings to consider what someone else is feeling. Ask the children to write a paragraph about something that happened between them and someone else. They need to write what they felt at that moment and what they think the other person was feeling.

Let's say they did something wrong and are grounded for a day. They must first write about how they feel about what happened. Then, they need to write about how the parent who grounded them feels about what happened.

Afterward, have a group discussion about expanding on their observations.

### *Group Circle*

Have the kids sit in a circle before introducing a certain topic for discussion. I recommend that you choose a topic that is relevant to them. In the group, there is only one object—you can use a soft toy, stick, or even a stone—what is important is that only the person with the object can speak.

Start by passing the object around in the circle so that everyone can check in. Once you introduce the topic, only the person with the object can express their feelings and thoughts related to the matter, and then they can pass it on to the next child they want to give it to. This way, there is only one speaker, and everyone else needs to listen.

## In Conclusion

Never underestimate the importance of empathy toward others in your home, your child's friendships, and even in the wider society. The ability to see what others feel and reach out to them in comforting understanding keeps the community in check.

All children are born with the ability to be empathetic, but you need to help your child to develop this skill as, initially, they may not care for the emotions of others. It means that you need to model the behavior you want your child to adopt, continuously help them practice their ability to read the emotions of others just by looking at them, and then, at a later stage, begin to think about what other people feel and why. The ability to place yourself in the shoes of another is vital to enjoying lasting friendships.

# 5

# HOW DO I MAKE DECISIONS?

> *"Decision-making skills teach preschoolers that actions have consequences, and we have to live with them."*
>
> — RAINFOREST LEARNING CENTRE INC.

Some people can make decisions with exceptional ease; for others, every time they reach a point where they have to decide on even the most insignificant things in life, they go into a tailspin as choices are just too hard for them to make. Raising kids who are confident in deciding things for themselves will surely benefit them during adulthood, but it is not the only reason you need to help your little ones grow comfortable with making choices. No, some of the worst friends to have are the ones with whom you make plans, then they never show up, or when they make decisions, they don't want to accept the consequences of these choices.

### Their Decisions Matter

I am not encouraging you to leave all the choices in your child's life up to them. That would be irresponsible parenting. But there are benefits to both your child and you to allowing them to make at least some choices for themselves. Giving even younger children this responsibility gives them confidence an immense boost, which is vital in parenting. Yet, you have far more benefits by allowing your child to decide between having grape juice or apple juice or whether they want to play with blocks or build puzzles. Yes, it is a sure way to minimize the number of tantrums in your home. Often, at the root of these emotional outbursts, you find frustration with their lack of control over their lives, and choices resolve this frustration. Coupled with the fact that you are boosting their self-esteem and increasing their self-worth, you also teach them to take responsibility for their lives. For example, if they've said that they don't want to go to grandma's place on their way home and you've checked with them that it was what they've decided, don't tolerate an outburst when you arrive home and they realize they didn't make this pitstop along the way. Lastly, giving your child this kind of freedom encourages them to be more creative as choices trigger abstract thinking.

Exposing your child to choices can take place from a very young age onwards. So, let's see how you can support your child in this regard.

### Babies (0-1 Year)

Babies may come across as helpless and unable to know what they want, right? Wrong.

**Babies Can Make Decisions?**

If your baby is crying and you can't seem to get them to calm down, it quickly becomes evident that even at this very young age, babies can distinguish between what they want and what they don't want. Additionally, they are very comfortable expressing their free will, and you will know very well that what you offer them is not what they want until their needs are satisfied.

**Step 1: Listen & Observe**

The challenge with your little one is not that they are indecisive; no, they are merely lacking the ability to communicate what they want. So, as the mommy or daddy on duty, you can help your child by observing them closely. Look and listen to learn what their preferences are when it comes to food and toys. What are the things your baby loves to explore, and which things don't interest them at all?

**Step 2: This or That**

Start by giving them small choices. Which soft toy do they want? What pair of clothing do they reach out to when you hold it up for them? What food do they reach for if you give them a choice? Once your baby makes a choice, remove the other out of sight.

**Step 3: Keep the Choices Safe!**

Keep these choices within healthy limits. When giving your little one an option, be sure that you'll be perfectly fine with what they've chosen. It doesn't matter to you which soft toy they prefer or what outfit they are choosing for the day because you've already pre-approved all options you offer.

**Step 4: "You Don't Like This?"**

Sometimes your baby makes it very clear that they don't like a certain option they are presented with by pushing away the object. When they do, acknowledge that they don't like it and say, "You don't want this," and then you can offer them something else.

**Step 5: No Clutter Around Baby**

Have you ever been to a store and then there were so many options to choose from you left without buying anything? The same is the case for your baby. If there are too many options for them to choose from, they'll find it very hard to pick anything. So, keep the area around them clutter-free.

**Step 6: Praise Their Choices**

Don't we all like to hear how great our choices are and how well we make decisions for ourselves? Your baby is no different. So, tell your baby how well they've chosen and how good they are at making choices, as this will leave them self-assured in their ability to select and increase their confidence.

**Step 7: Model Planning**

Here, too, you can model the correct behavior for your baby. While your baby may not be able to grasp everything you say to them yet, you can still talk them through the decision-making process. Share a decision you have to make with your baby and go through the entire process. For example, "Mommy needs to go to work, but Mommy doesn't feel like going today. If Mommy doesn't go and stay home, we can have fun, but if Mommy does go, I'll be able to earn money, which will help me buy everything my baby needs." Any similar sample will work and use your discretion regarding what you share with your baby. Always remember that even while they are so little still, they are way more observant than we think.

**Toddlers (1-3 Years)**

Your approach regarding decision-making is the same between this stage and the previous one.

**Step 1: This or That?**

Again, give your baby choices, but always pre-approve all the options you offer. For example, do you want to wear pink socks or purple socks?

**Step 2: Explain Your Choices**

You are giving your child certain choices, but you can't give them free rein over all the decisions. Therefore, it is bound to happen that there will be times when your little one's choices may be in conflict with yours. In these instances, it is best to explain your options as these explanations start to create the foundation to understand that options have good reasons. For example, let's say your kid only wants to eat cereal and shows a strong resistance toward vegetables. This is not a choice you've left for them to decide. Therefore, you have to tell your child that vegetables aren't as tasty as cereal but will help them grow into a big boy or girl and keep them healthy. So, they need to eat it.

**Step 3: Learn Their Interests**

The more observant you are of your child's behavior, the more familiar you'll get with their interests. Yes, they already have specific preferences and interests, even at such a young age. Use these to guide them through the decision-making process. For example, let's say little Kyle doesn't want to wear his jacket; he can't go outside to play ball. If he wants to do what he likes—kicking a ball—then he needs to make choices that will allow him to do it.

**Step 4: Keep Things Tidy!**

Again, making decisions when overwhelmed with many things in our environment distracting us is hard enough as an adult. Just imagine how challenging it must be if you are still so young. Help your little one to make decisions with greater ease by keeping their environment tidy.

**Step 5: Talk About Books**

Reading remains a powerful way to teach. Choose age-appropriate stories about characters that had to make choices or even who made choices that worked out well or not so well. The reality is that not all options are good, and your child needs to learn how to deal with these moments too.

**Step 6: Play Games!**

Learning should be fun, and there are many games you can play to help your child understand the importance of choices and how to make good ones. So, at the end of the chapter, I am sharing some fun but effective choices.

**Step 7: Get Ready to Swoop In**

Your toddler may be keen to make certain choices, and you support this quest. Yet, when the moment arrives, and they need to decide, it can be overwhelming, and they don't know what to choose. This is when mommy or daddy needs to be ready to swoop in and, without taking over, guide them to decide.

**Preschoolers (3-5 Years)**

By now, your child has a greater understanding of choices, which means that if they've chosen one thing, they can't just change their mind willy-nilly later.

**Step 1: Let's Talk About It**

It also means you can sit them down now and discuss their options. Did you enjoy the choice you made by having a strawberry milkshake rather than bubblegum? You can also help them work through the process when they have to decide certain things. You can upper questions like:

- Do you want to go to Sarah's party?
- What will happen if you don't go?
- How will you feel if all your friends are there and you're not?

These will help your little one to think a bit further than merely giving a yes or no answer, an answer they'll likely regret later.

**Step 2: Involve Them!**

Get your child's input on the decisions you need to make. For example, mommy is unsure whether to wear a green or a black dress. What do you think? When they give their answer, you can even ask them why. But, again, be sure to be fine with a response that goes either way when it comes to these choices. Ultimately, you do want them to see that you follow their advice.

**Step 3: What Do We Know?**

Before making any important decisions, you need to find as much information as possible to make an informed choice. Your child is ready to learn this lesson now too. When they are posed with an option to make, ask them what they know about the situation and how this information is impacting their choices. I want us to revert to the party invite. Who will be at the party? Are these kids friends you like to play with? Do you think you'll enjoy playing with them at the party? Keep the questions short and simple not to confuse your child while still guiding them to make a confident choice.

**Step 4: Keep Asking Questions**

Teach your child that if they aren't sure about their choice, they should ask more questions and gain more information. This way, they may find information to guide them in making the best choice.

**Step 5: Play More Games!**

Again, games make learning fun. Explore the selection of fun games presented at the end of the chapter.

### Step 6: What's Going to Happen?

When the information they have isn't enough to guide them along the way, it may be necessary to look at how different choices will work out. Again, it is party time, and your child needs to decide whether they want to go or not. What will happen if you go? What will happen if you don't? These questions encourage their young minds to think beyond the actual moment and consider their choices' effects. Learning this is vital to becoming good decision-makers in life.

### Step 7: Pros & Cons

Your kid is old enough to realize that specific outcomes are good, and others are not. To them, it boils down to which option they would rather have. It means your child needs to decide based on every choice's pros and cons. Remember, highlighting the cons of any choice should never be confused with fear-mongering. You don't want to raise the stakes so high that they become scared of making any choices. However, you do want them to know that every choice has the potential to turn out either way.

### Elementary Schoolers (5-10 Years)

By now, your kids have a solid understanding of decision-making processes and that choices have consequences. From now onwards, you can support them in strengthening their decision-making skills. The best you can do at this stage is regularly walk your child through the entire decision process.

**Step 1: What's Wrong? What Needs to Be Done?**

Identify the problem they are facing. Friends play an essential role in your child's life at this age, so having a friend who does not want to play with them at school will be a big deal to them. What can they do about it? What choices are they left with to resolve the concern they are facing?

**Step 2: What Do We Know?**

What information do they need to make an informed choice? Help your kid determine exactly why it happened. Did they do something to cause this reaction in the friend? Highlight that they can only make good decisions if they have all the necessary information.

**Step 3: What Can We Do?**

Help them identify who they can ask for information or how they'll gain the insights they need to make an informed choice. Then, run through several options with your child. For example, they can leave the situation as it is and see if the friend will return to them, or they can decide to ask the friend what happened and restore the friendship. Maybe you can even set up a playdate afterschool.

**Step 4: What's Going to Happen If...**

Now they should be clear on the options they have. So, help your child consider every option's pros and cons. What will happen if they do nothing? Will they be apologizing for something they didn't do, perhaps? Will they lose their friend? Are they willing to lose a friend?

**Step 5: Make a Choice**

Encourage your child to make a decision based on the information they have. By now, all the information available should be on the table, and your child should decide what they think is best to do.

**Step 6: Time to Move!**

Once the decision is made, it is final. Encourage your kid to stick to the choices they've made. If they don't, they'll only start to doubt their choices later, leading to indecisiveness at a later stage in life. If they've decided to do nothing, that is what they should stick to, but if your child chooses to reach out to the friend, that should be done first thing when they see the friend again.

**Step 7: So, What Happened?**

Once they've taken action, sit them down and discuss their choice's outcome. Did it work out well? If so, praise their decision-making skills. If not, help them to see what they can do better next time. This conversation will most likely take place after school the next day. Ask your child how it went. Are they friends again? Or if the friend didn't cooperate, how did that make your kid feel? Advise your child how to move on if it doesn't work out as they wish.

**Middle Schoolers (10+)**

This is an exciting time as you can now introduce your child to decision-making techniques, they'll be able to use in their adult life too.

**Step 1: Introduce SMART Goal Setting**

Choices should always be aligned with goals. Your child is old enough to introduce them to SMART goals and guide them to make SMART goals for their lives. SMART goals are specific, measurable, achievable, realistic, and timely.

**Step 2: "Is That the Only Option?"**

Sometimes, especially when our kids find themselves in a real pickle, it may appear like they have no options. This can be a frustrating position to be in and can leave them feeling trapped. Help them to explore what other choices the specific situation may have. Encourage creative thinking to see solutions rather than problems. Once they have identified more options, let them explore the pros and cons of every choice.

**Step 3: Let Them Know You Trust Them**

Knowing that you are still loved even if you make mistakes is one of the greatest ways to build your kid's confidence. Therefore, remind your child that you trust their decisions and that regardless of how it works out, you are still there for them and love them dearly. When things work out well, remember to praise them. And when it doesn't, validate their feelings. Empathize with your child and guide them to see how they can do better next time.

**Step 4: "Remember the Pros & Cons?"**

Your child is now old enough to draft a list of pros and cons. Creating such a list makes it more evident which option is best. But how can you apply this practically? Stop making it your concern when your child doesn't want to do their homework.

Instead, ask them to draft a list of pros and cons if they don't do what is expected of them. Then, when they still make the wrong choice, they must face the consequences of their decisions. It may sound harsh but rather have them learn these lessons under your roof than when they are already out in the big world.

**Step 5: There's Always a Place for No**

Even though you allow your child to make certain choices for themselves, you must remain the person who can veto all of them. This is not control you hold onto to disempower them but to protect them. Children may be very independent, but they don't have the life experience of an adult. Rather have an angry child on your hands for a while than deal with far more severe consequences.

**Step 6: Let's Talk Money...**

When your child reaches this stage, money will likely play an important role in their choices. Therefore, by allowing them to make certain choices linked to money and guiding them to manage these choices well, they'll become money-wise too.

**Step 7: Let Them Make Mistakes**

We all make mistakes. Thank goodness for that, as it is the best way for us to learn. Rather than criticizing your child for their mistakes while making choices, explain to them that we all do it at some time in our lives. The only way to improve is to see how you can learn from your mistakes and consider a better option next time.

## ACTIVITIES

### Let's Make Decisions!

Are you ready to help your kids to become excellent at making decisions? The following activities will make teaching decision-making skills fun!

### Babies

#### *This or That?*

While it is never too early to start, you are still somewhat limited in what you can do at this stage in your child's life. Regularly presenting choices is the best and most fun activity for your little ones. This soft toy or that one? These socks or those? This top or that one? Always hold up both options and watch your baby closely to see which one they prefer.

### Toddlers

#### *Memory Game*

I love this game as it brings more benefits than you've been hoping for. It helps your child's decision-making skills and triggers their memory.

Use a set of cards that contains matching pictures and place them upside down. Take turns choosing two cards to turn around. If the pictures of the cards match, you keep them; if not, they need to be turned back face down, and it is the other person's turn to play. Continue until all the cards have been used, and the player with the most cards wins. You can play this game with only two players or more. Can you see this game give your child options, teach them to wait their turn, and encourage them to remember which cards were where to help them win?

## Preschoolers

### *How the Story Goes*

The game offers a fun and creative way to end the day. At bedtime, read only the first couple of pages of a story your child is unfamiliar with. Then you can give them two options of how the story may continue, and your child needs to choose one option. For example, the little girl met a prince who protected her against the evil dragon. Or the little girl learned how to use a sword and fought and won against the evil dragon.

### *Musical Chairs*

This game can be played in a group or when you have a couple of kids over for a play date. It teaches kids to make choices and to do so quickly.

Start by having a chair for every kid lined up in the room. They can run around while music is playing, but the moment the music stops, they all need to find a chair.

Remove one chair and play the music. Once it stops, one kid will be without a chair. That kid falls out. Repeat the process until there are only two players and one chair left. The one who gets the chair the last time wins.

## Elementary Schoolers

### *Pick Up Sticks*

This game is as old as the mountains, so I am sure you know how to play it. But still, just a quick recap. Hold the sticks above a table or the floor and drop them into a pile. Every kid gets a turn to pick up a stick without letting any of the other sticks move. You are out if you move a stick from the pile while picking up your chosen stick. Therefore, you need to consider all your choices before deciding on what stick to pick up. The winner is the player with the most sticks.

***3-in-a-Row, Tic Tac Toe!***

Also known as noughts and crosses, you are familiar with the game too. You need two players, each with a symbol assigned to them. Then it would help if you drew the framework to play, two parallel horizontal lines crossing two parallel vertical lines. The goal is to get three of the same symbols in a line, vertically, horizontally, or diagonally. Players need to prevent the other player from doing this while working on getting their symbols lined up like this. So, it requires making smart choices quickly.

### Middle Schoolers

***Monopoly Junior***

Another classic game from your childhood years. Monopoly requires strategic thinking, and the winner is the one who makes the smartest choices. The game also involves effective use and spending of money and can be played by only two players or the entire family.

***Would You Rather?***

The game supports decision-making skills but also creative thinking. It can be played with only two players or many, and the game's beauty is that you can play it anywhere to make time pass faster. It consists of asking questions like:

- Would you rather be a bird or a bat?
- Would you rather eat a worm or a snail?
- Would you rather want to be rich or strong?
- Would you rather have many friends or good friends?

Players can ask questions to gather more information regarding their choices, and then they need to choose and state why they decided on the specific option.

### In Conclusion

Being great decision-makers will help your children choose friends who are good for them, while making confident choices is a social strength that will benefit your child even into adulthood.

It is a skill you can start teaching your kids from early onwards as even babies can express their likes and dislikes in life. Therefore, it is never too late to start guiding your child on making choices that will benefit them.

# 6

# HOW DO I DEAL WITH BULLIES?

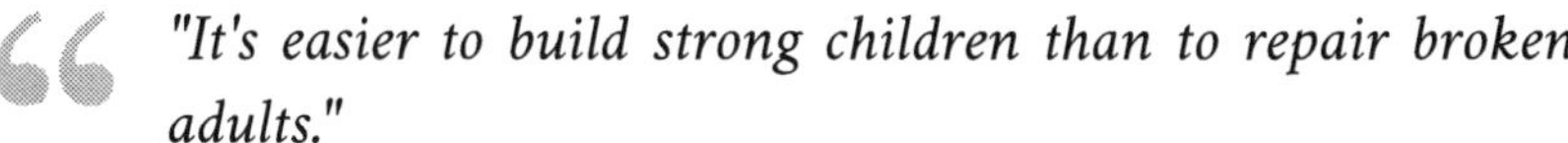

> *"It's easier to build strong children than to repair broken adults."*
>
> — FREDERICK DOUGLAS

The word bully is a nightmare for every parent and teacher across the globe. Unfortunately, bullying can become part of your child's life, threatening their physical, mental, and emotional well-being. However, the reality is that bullies aren't only a threat on the school grounds, and your kids may become victims of cyberbullying later in life. That said, bullies can also be found in office cubicles and around boardroom tables. It is never too early to start preparing your child to protect themselves against bullies and, importantly, to guide them never to become bullies themselves.

### Babies (0-1 Year) & Toddlers (1-3 Years)

At this stage, your kids are likely too little to have bullies in their lives. That said, they may come across people they may consider to be mean. Therefore, there is no reason to delay preparing your child for dealing with kids who are mean to them. You also don't want your child ever to portray such behavior.

#### Step 1: Educate Them About "Meanies"

As your little one is still so young, they may be more familiar with the term *meanies* than with bullies. However, even though they may not be bullied or witness bullying, they will surely come across mean kids at the playground or park. Meanies would be kids who always grab every toy, only want to play games they like, never give anyone a turn, or would say ugly things to other kids. As this behavior can cause your child to withdraw from play, you would want your child to identify such behavior early on and make you aware of these incidents at school.

#### Step 2: Encourage Open, Constant Communication

While trust can be broken in seconds, it is built over time. Even when it comes to your kids, whom you may feel should naturally trust you, it can require time to establish the foundation of open communication, encouraging them to share every detail of their day with you. The older kids get, the harder it becomes to establish such a foundation, so instead, start young and ask your child daily how their days were. You'll have to listen carefully when they share their days to pick up on anything that might have upset them, for initially, they may not share these incidents. However, always encourage your little one to tell you if someone was mean to them during the day.

### Step 3: Teach Them How to Spot a Bully

How do you spot a bully? While this seems to be a simple question, the answer is sometimes much more complex than anticipated. It can be easy to convince yourself that maybe you've perceived the situation all wrong. Now imagine how much harder it is for your little ones still so young. By asking the following questions, you can help your child to identify meanies or bullies:

- Did the other kid hurt you on purpose?
- How many times did they do that to you?
- How did that make you feel? Angry? Hurt? Sad?
- Did the kid know they hurt you?
- Is the other kid bigger or stronger than you?

### Step 4: Teach Them the SILT Strategy

My kids were still very young when I had drilled it into their little heads to say no. Yet saying no is only the first step in the SILT strategy, and your child can benefit from knowing all four steps:

- **S**ay no to bullies and clarify that you want them to stop.
- **I**gnore your bullies and try your best not to react
- **L**eave the bully and walk away from the situation.
- **T**ell your teacher or any other adult what happened to you.

### Step 5: Encourage Them to Foster Friendship

Bullies come across as strong and brave, but in my experience, they are actually weaklings. Therefore, they prefer to bully kids who can be described as loners, hence the concern about your child's well-being if they don't make friends. So, the best protection your child can have is to be surrounded by a group of close friends. When you encourage this, you are already helping your child to build a barrier to keeping them safe when you aren't around.

**Step 6: Create Bullying Responses**

Your child's first response toward bullying will likely determine whether this will become a repeat event. Teaching your little one appropriate ways to respond to such mean behavior can prevent them from falling victim to school bullies. You can practice this exercise at home with roleplay to prepare your child and prevent them from being overwhelmed the first time they encounter a bully. Be sure to include what you want them to do after such an incident and who they must tell immediately to take care of the matter.

**Step 7: Build Their Confidence**

Bullies lack confidence; therefore, they'll always single out the kids who are visibly lacking in this area too. As this is the case, confidence is the best protective shield you can offer your child. So always boost their confidence to keep them safe.

### Preschoolers (3-5 Years), Elementary (5-10 Years) & Middle Schoolers (10+)

Bullying is a serious matter, and it should never be considered harmless fun. It may appear harmless fun from a distance, but believe me, it is never how the bullied child perceives their situation. Therefore, I am diverting a bit from the structure I've followed up until this point as there are several sides and many people impacted by such an event. It is necessary to address the parent's concerns about the child being bullied and the child's needs and to advise parents whose kids have become bullies on how to handle the matter best.

## My Child is Being Bullied

Being in this position is both heartbreaking and frustrating. You can see your child is hurt, but you don't always know how to help your child best. It is a space filled with mixed emotions as you are so angry at the bully that you want to march right up to them and sort them out, but you know that will only worsen the situation. Then you may also feel that your child must be a bit stronger and stand up for themselves, but at the same time, you are feeling immensely sorry for them over what they are going through, and you are worried about what this is doing to them. I am not even going into your frustration, as it can come across as if the system and school are failing you and your child. Lastly, a little bit of disgust is growing inside of you, rooted in the blame you shift toward this kid's parents—a complex situation.

### Step 1: Listen to What Your Child Is Saying

Raising kids without a clear and trusted communication channel is almost impossible. Therefore, it is so vital that you set the foundation for trusted communication from an early age onwards. A large part of good communication consists of your ability to listen to what your child has to say. Listening attentively when they tell you about their day lets you pick up on matters that upset them. By asking how you can help them, you open the door for them to share more about these incidents. Remember to keep your cool. If you are going to be visibly upset about what your child is telling you, they may be more reserved to share similar information again.

### Step 2: Listen to What Your Child Isn't Saying

That said, the second step is listening so well that you can also pick up on what they don't say. Sometimes not saying certain things is as revealing as telling everything about them. You need to concentrate, watch your child's body language, and remain aware of the entire conversation to be sure you don't miss out on vital information not shared verbally. My advice to parents is that if something feels off in their gut, trust it, explore it, and determine what bothers them about a specific situation.

### Step 3: Ask Questions & Encourage Honesty

This is especially true when you feel that something is off about the situation, whether your child is telling you all about it or not. Ask all the questions you need to ask to gain the clarity you must have as a parent, and while doing so, encourage your child that you will do the right thing for them and what is in their best interest. Sometimes kids want to share what has happened, but they don't want their parents to become so upset that they cause a scene at their schools the next day. If your child is slightly older, ask them how they want you to help them, and don't only jump in to address the matter as you see best fit. Remember, your child is much more familiar with their world's social cues and dynamics than you, so give their opinion the value it deserves.

### Step 4: Work on a Response Together

Instead of taking control of the matter, offer your help and make this a team effort. By working with your child and devising a plan to end this behavior, you increase your kid's confidence in their ability to take care of themselves rather than disempowering them by taking control of everything. In addition, you bring life experience to the table, and they get the wisdom of their situation. Together you can be a winning team coming up with a brilliant solution to put an end to bullying.

**Step 5: Talk to the Bully's Parents**

When you've already tried several ways to resolve the concern amicably, and there is still no improvement in the intimidation your child is suffering, reaching out to the bully's parents becomes necessary. In such a meeting, you'll be able to determine whether you can work together to find a solution. However, please don't go into this meeting emotionally charged and ready to accuse them of everything. It is their child who is a bully, not them who are intimidating your child. Instead, asking them for their help and suggestions on how they feel would be a good way to stop their child's behavior.

**Step 6: Work with the Teachers/School**

The sad reality is that when you meet the bully's parents, it quickly becomes evident that the apple doesn't fall far from the tree, and you instantly know they won't offer cooperation. While this is disappointing, to say the very least, you aren't left in a helpless situation. No, now you can put more pressure on the school to address the manner through their formal systems and structures. Every school or formal body has a written code of conduct, and you may have to press teachers or the school principal to escalate matters in the legally prescribed way—even if it results in suspension for the other kid. Your child remains your priority, and you must do what it takes to keep them safe.

### Step 7: Get Support for Yourself

As you get so consumed by worrying over your child and the negative impact the situation has on them, you may completely neglect to notice how it impacts you. You are also emotionally disturbed by what your child is going through, and as you must remain strong and calm for your kid's sake, it is helpful and recommendable that you get the support you need too. This can either be through a friend or having someone willing to listen. If you don't have such good friends or don't want to burden others with your problems, it will help to see a professional for guidance, support, and advice.

## I'm Being Bullied

It is tough to say in advance how you'll react when you are being bullied for the very first time. While some kids are in shock or hurt, maybe even angry, over what just happened, others aren't sure whether it was just how they perceived the moment and whether the other child was bullying them. It is mainly the latter that is my concern, as this doubt in your ability to judge what happened to you doesn't do your confidence any good and makes you even more vulnerable to a repeat of the situation. So, it is why I want you to take the following steps, even if you are in doubt, okay?

### Step 1: Tell Your Teacher & Parents, No Matter What

Being bullied is a serious concern and not something you should ever try to deal with alone. It is why it is so important that you immediately talk to someone you trust, like a parent or a teacher. This person will have an outside perspective on the matter, and it will be easier for them to know the right thing to do as they are less emotional about what happened. It will also make you feel better once you've shared your feelings with someone else.

**Step 2: "Back Off!"**

This is just one of the many responses you can give to the bully next time they approach you. These phrases should state clearly that you don't like what they do and will not stand for being treated this way. Yet, you don't want to tempt the bully even further, so choose statements that make it clear that you disapprove of their behavior without pushing them to respond even further. Rather walk away and create distance between yourself and the bully.

**Step 3: Use the Buddy System**

Bathrooms, locker rooms, and quiet spots on the playground are the places bullies like to wait for those they torment. They know that these are all places they'll be able to find you alone and where nobody will see them bullying you. So, protect yourself when going to these places. Be smart, and don't go to the bathroom if you know the bully is nearby. Or you can use the buddy system and be sure that you have someone you trust going along with you. The bully is far less likely to do something when you are accompanied by someone you trust.

**Step 4: Just Ignore Them (If You Can)**

Every time a bully confronts you, the situation can be different. It is why it is best to have a range of possible responses or reactions up your sleeve. So, as I advise here to ignore the bully and walk away, this may not be the best response for every situation. You may not feel safe enough to turn your back on the bully but take it if the situation leans itself to this reaction. Don't engage in the bully's attempts to get a reaction out of you.

**Step 5: It's Okay to Be Upset**

Don't beat yourself up about being so upset over what happened. Bullies intentionally violate your human rights and want you to show this kind of reaction. Even though you did your best not to show the bully how big their impact on you was, you may still be extremely upset over what happened for days afterward. It is okay to feel this way. However, rather than ignoring your feelings, acknowledge them, embrace them as normal, and find ways to deal with them productively. It will also help when your parents or teachers understand what you are going through and are willing to help you.

**Step 6: Don't Retaliate**

You feel like you need to stand up for yourself, right? You want to get back at the bully; hurt them as they hurt you. You want them to taste their own medicine, don't you? Of course, you do. Who wouldn't feel this way? But this is the worst response you can have. Remember that bullies are weaklings, and they come in packs. If you choose to respond, you will not be up against only the bully but also the kid's entire pack. It is an unfair fight. Don't step into it blindly. I've too often seen how bullies get away with what they do to kids as they do this out of sight, but the moment their victims retaliate with words or actions, they are spotted and get themselves into trouble at school. Instead, follow the correct procedures and report these events immediately.

### Step 7: It's Not Your Fault, Okay?

There are ways to change your body language and ways to become less inviting to a bully, but that said, by no means does it ever mean that it was your fault that a bully singled you out. Nobody deserves to be bullied for how they walk, talk, or anything else. By allowing yourself to feel guilty and as if it is your fault, you are playing right into the bully's hands, so just don't.

## My Child Is a Bully

This, too, can be an awful position to find yourself in. However, I don't think any parent deliberately raises their kids to become bullies. Sometimes, some life lessons get lost in translation; your child may perceive the life wisdom you've shared entirely wrong and apply it unacceptably. But in most of the cases, this miscommunication didn't take place intentionally. Still, it is a matter of great concern, and you need to address it appropriately if your child is guilty of bullying.

### Step 1: Take it Seriously

I often hear parents state things like, "You know, boys will be boys." I find this to be quite insulting to the feelings and intelligence of the victim of a bullying incident. Bullying is not a stage kids go through at some time in their lives. No, it is often an outcry for help because, in many instances, this behavior either indicates more profound emotional scars in the bully or can even cause them more hurt than their victims may experience. Bullies don't outgrow this kind of behavior. If the matter isn't addressed, your child will only grow into an adult who doesn't mind hurting others.

**Step 2: Talk to Them ASAP**

The longer you know about this behavior and don't do something about it, the more it will look like you approve of it. This will only make changing your child's behavior much harder when matters get out of hand. So, as soon as you are alerted of what is happening in your child's life, you need to address the concern. It is also important to remember that the longer your child is keeping up with this behavior, the more other parent's kids are getting hurt.

**Step 3: Determine the Why**

It is never the case that a child wakes up one day and turns into a bully. No, there is always a reason your child behaves this way. Often this behavior is an outcry for help, an expression of anger, or even modeled behavior they observe at home. Yet, these aren't the only reasons for kids to turn into bullies, but one thing is sure, all bullies do it for a reason, and often, it is because they need help too. So, please give your child the support they need to keep them from spreading the hurt or anger they feel to other kids too.

**Step 4: Remind Them That Bullying is a Choice, And Choices Have...**

There are different ways to act out and release a build-up of anger or hurt. If your child chooses to bully to eliminate their negative emotions, you need to emphasize that this is a choice and choices can be changed. Choices should be changed, especially if it has such a negative impact on the lives of others. Encourage your child to accept responsibility for their actions and guide them to more constructive ways to deal with their emotions.

**Step 5: Appropriate Consequences**

Actions have consequences—I've mentioned the importance of this already in an earlier chapter. If your child chooses to be a bully, their behavior is going to have consequences. You, as the parent, need to determine what these consequences will be at home. When they display this behavior at school—which is usually the case—they'll also face the consequences. Still, it would be best to address the matter at home. Determine what punishment would best fit the crime. For example, if your child used their position on the first sports team to intimate or bully others, take that privilege away from them or inform their coach that they won't be playing in the next game or two. Cyberbullying is a major concern in our modern society. If your child is guilty of this type of bullying, a suitable punishment would be to take away all their electronic devices.

**Step 6: Work with the School & Parents Involved**

The most effective manner to address bullying is to work with the school and the parents of the victim. These parents aren't your enemies and seeing them in a similar light will only reinforce your child's idea that you are now in a situation of us against them. This is not the kind of mentality you want to promote. Instead, model cooperative behavior and see how you can contribute to resolving the matter as quickly and painlessly as possible.

**Step 7: Monitor the Situation as Long as Possible**

Without hovering over your child's every move, remain aware of their behavior or actions. As soon as you whiff that they are again behaving similarly, nip the problem in the bud and immediately reach out to the involved parties to collaborate with you on addressing the concern.

### Stories

Unless you've been bullied, it is almost impossible to put yourself in the shoes of these victims. Bullying is the kind of behavior that may leave visible scars, but the more concerning factors are the invisible marks left on the lives of these victims. These are scars caused by feelings of rejection, humiliation, worthlessness, and being ostracized. It is the kind of behavior that occurs during a life stage when having friends and being socially accepted plays a key role in personal development, and these kids are robbed of this opportunity.

The other majorly concerning factor of bullying is that it repeats itself daily. It is not like being mugged in the street; it was an event that happened once and is over. Oh no, every day that the child goes to school, they know they will be faced with their bully. They will be humiliated, hurt, rejected, and made fun of at their cost. They know that each instance will have onlookers, but no heroes are coming to save them. They are on their own in this misery.

Speaking to many victims of bullying years or even decades after this traumatizing time, it becomes evident that they are still carrying the scars of this time along with them into adulthood. Many feel it is hard to forgive their bully as they've never been served an apology. Forgiving someone who doesn't even show remorse for what they've done is exceptionally challenging. Yet, if this is you, if you find yourself on the receiving end of bullying, I also want to encourage you by stating that life does get better. You can heal again and that, with enough time, you can be free from the emotional burden of being bullied.

## In Conclusion

The tragedy of bullying should be avoided at all costs. It is the kind of behavior that doesn't only negatively impact the life of the victim but also of the bully. As parents, it is heartbreaking to see our kids go through this lasting misery and heartache, but there is a lot you can do to prepare your child and keep them safe from this kind of behavior. We've explored bullying and ways to address it from all angles. However, the most important step you can ever take is to assure your child of their worth and boost their confidence.

# 7

# HOW CAN I BE CONFIDENT?

*"My father gave me the greatest gift anyone could give another person; he believed in me."*

— JIM VALVANO

If there is only one thing you can send your kids off with into the world, what will that one thing be? For me, the one thing I'll choose, as I believe that it will never run out, always help them to achieve their dreams and goals, and help them to overcome hardships and challenges, is confidence. Yes, confidence in the fact that they are loved, good enough, and capable of achieving whatever they've set out to do. While I want them to take that into adulthood, confidence and building this belief start at a very young age. So, yes, you can already start now, or let me rephrase, you must start now to build the foundation for healthy confidence to exist and grow within your kids.

### What Is Self-Esteem?

The term self-esteem refers to your perception of your worth or value as a person. The term is linked to your sense of identity and belonging, how competent you feel to do certain things, how secure you feel in your position, and how confident you are in your relationships but also in general. These are all factors influencing the state of your self-esteem but are also impacted by it.

### 3 Types of Self-Esteem

There are three types of self-esteem, each referring to its specific state and how well you think of yourself.

- **Inflated self-esteem** may be good because you never doubt your abilities and are confident in what you are capable of, but it also indicates that you think you are better than others. This perception of being above others hurts your relationships and makes you socially less likable. Forming strong and meaningful bonds with those who see themselves in this light is very hard.
- **Low self-esteem** is at the opposite end of the spectrum, and it refers to a state where you don't value yourself at all. Your insecurities constantly impact your life, and even the slightest challenge may be daunting, overwhelming you. This, too, will strain your social connections and relationships.
- **High self-esteem** is just perfect. You value yourself, trust your abilities to take on challenges, and maintain a positive outlook in life. You consider other people your equals and respect them for it, while you never doubt your ability to excel.

**Why Self-Esteem Matters**

The more you believe in your ability to achieve your goals, the happier your life becomes and the easier it is to overcome obstacles, make friends, and achieve your goals. Likewise, your kids' ability to do well at school, have friends, be happy, and be a pleasure at home are all directly linked to their self-esteem.

**Babies (0-1 Year)**

You can already begin laying the foundation for your child's healthy confidence at this young age, as babies are so sensitive toward their environment and how they are treated.

**Step 1: Make Sure They Know They're Safe & Secure**

The most important thing for your little one is to ensure they feel secure. As they are so vulnerable, security and having them feel protected and confident that you are there for them when they need you is vital. When your baby cries, attend to their needs, create a friendly and safe home environment, and give them all the love they need to feel safe and protected.

**Step 2: Always Be on Standby to Give Big Hugs**

Being around to give love and kisses is another way to leave your little one confident that you're always there for them and that they are accepted and loved in a secure environment. So, love, hug, and kiss them. This is good for you and them.

**Step 3: "You Found Mommy!"**

Play games with your little one, like peek-a-boo, as this provides the opportunity to praise them for their achievements. Through praise, you instill a sense of confidence. It can be praise for things like finding mommy, standing up, crawling, or even holding a spoon.

**Step 4: Model Confidence & Persistence**

You are always the role model, so be aware of what you do and how you react when your baby sees you, for they truly do see you in every possible way and will always follow the example mommy or daddy is giving them.

**Step 5: Establish Routines**

Having certainty about what is happening adds a little comfort to all our lives. For us, it is easy to check our diary or run to the to-do list pinned on the fridge door; for them, they need to find this security and confidence in routines. By maintaining a specific eat-bath-bed routine, your little one knows what is coming next when you feed them, as they know after bathing; it is bedtime. This establishes a calming confidence in your child.

**Step 6: "You Did That! That Makes Mommy Happy!"**

While praise is good and encourages your child's confidence to grow, expressing how your baby's achievements make you feel is also beneficial. You, too, like to know that when you've done well, it makes others feel good. Your baby is no different.

**Step 7: "Look How Far You've Come!"**

Sometimes it will require quite a bit of patience from you to let your baby do the same things over and over. Yet, every time they do something again, explore the same thing again, or go through the same processes, they observe new features and even learn new things about themselves. Your encouragement to keep this up is surely setting the pathway for them to proceed even further.

**Toddlers (1-3 Years)**

At this stage, your approach to increasing confidence in your little one isn't much different from the previous one, but I recommend that you focus on the following points.

**Step 1: Show Unconditional Love, No Matter What**

Love feeds the soul, and the certainty that they are being loved unconditionally gives your kids the security they need to thrive in life. Show them you love them with hugs, kisses, cuddles, and quality time. It is how you have your kids feel loved and assure them that they matter.

**Step 2: Praise Their Perseverance**

We all love to get attention from our loved ones. I know for sure I do. So, what do we do to get this attention? We take action, depending on which action gets the best response from those whose attention we want, which is what we'll continue doing. So, if you want your child to persevere, praise them when they show this side of their personality. Kids crave attention far more than we do. If you aren't going to praise them and give them your attention when they do well in life, they will try to draw your attention by doing the complete opposite, for, in the end, attention is attention, regardless of whether it is good or bad.

**Step 3: Celebrate Their Efforts**

This step is closely linked to the previous and is almost the sequel to step 2. The difference is that not only will you praise your kid, but now you'll also tell others about how well they do. Yes, I am encouraging you to show off a little about your child, and the best time to do it is when they are within hearing distance. Try it and see how your little ones start to shine.

**Step 4: But Don't Overpraise**

That said, I also want to highlight that there is a limit within which you need to stick when it comes to praising too. If you praise them too much, one of two things can happen. First, they may either start to feel that if a bit of perseverance gets them this much praise, then they don't have to do much to get some praise, and this may lead to a deterioration in their behavior. Second, if you go overboard with your praising, it can come across as fake, and then they may not trust any praising anymore, for it just doesn't feel real any longer. So, yes, please praise but do so within reasonable limits.

**Step 5: Give Them a Chance to Say No**

There is no point in forcing your child into saying yes and being courageous all the time, and it is never the case that they do it because they chose to do so themselves. Therefore, allow them to say no, giving them time to make the conscious decision to be courageous and not step into the role by default.

**Step 6: Set Them Up for Success Sometimes**

While challenges will help your child realize their capabilities, these should be balanced against opportunities. You can do this by getting involved and creating instances for them when it will be easy to be courageous. For example, maybe your child feels more comfortable in the school concert because they know you are always there as part of the backstage crew. Honestly, this can be anything, but sometimes create instances where they can be successful with less effort.

**Step 7: Encourage & Appreciate Creativity**

For the longest time, I almost forgot the color of my fridge as it was entirely covered with my kids' drawings stuck onto the outside. This situation is not unique to my home, and I am sure you, too, have plenty of your kids' artwork up in your home. Having your child's artwork up for all to see serves as an excellent encouragement for them to explore further and develop their creative side, giving them confidence in their ability to create and to receive recognition for their work.

**Preschoolers (3-5 Years)**

This is a crucial time in your little one's life. Soon they'll take the giant leap forward of entering the formal schooling system, a system which can be demanding and even harsh on kids with low confidence in their abilities to excel.

**Step 1: Pay Undivided Attention**

How do you feel when you are talking to a loved one, and you don't have their full attention? Annoyed, irritated, or even that you don't mean that much to them? I know I surely get slightly hot around the collar when that happens. Now, imagine being your child's age and the person you depend on to care for your every need doesn't have the time to listen to you. That must suck, right? The suck that gives your confidence one nasty blow. So therefore, listen to your kids and give them your full attention.

**Step 2: Set Limits & Expect Them to Respect Them**

Whether you call them limits or rules, every home, school, organization, or company across the globe has these guidelines to ensure everything runs smoothly. Familiarize your kids with these limits and set the expectation that they should abide by these rules. Yes, for sure, they'll overstep these boundaries from time to time but continue to confirm your belief in their ability to do what is right.

**Step 3: Let Them Help!**

When was the last time you took on a challenge that you thought you might be unable to and then did? How did that make you feel? Confident in your abilities, perhaps? For sure! So, let your kids experience the same confidence boost by giving them tasks to care for at home and see how they flourish too. For example, give them a cloth to clean up a mess they've made or ask them to feed the family pet.

**Step 4: Assign Them Chores/Responsibilities**

Except for tasks you can hand to them during the day, you can also give them certain responsibilities to take care of, like feeding the family dog daily. Other tasks can be picking up their toys, placing their dirty laundry in the basket, and making their beds. While these will all give your kid a sense of accomplishment, boosting their confidence, it also offers you an opportunity to praise them for doing so well when they've taken care of all they have to do.

**Step 5: Let Them Make Their Own Choices**

In chapter five, we discussed the steps you could take to help your preschooler improve at making decisions. Reverting to these steps as one of the positives that flow from effective decision-making gives you confidence in yourself and the ability to make decisions.

**Step 6: Play with Them–And Let Them Lead!**

The satisfaction of winning is another fantastic boost for the confidence levels of young and old. You can create opportunities for your kids to experience this satisfaction by playing games—if they can choose which game to play, it is even better—and let them win. Give your child the overhand in a controlled environment, like with a board game or just throwing a ball in the garden, and see how they radiate confidence that ripples into other areas of their lives too.

**Step 7: "We Lost." "But Did You Have Fun?"**

Sure, winning is a significant confidence boost, but you can't allow losing to crush your confidence. So, what if your team has lost a game, or your kid fell out of a competition? What can you do to prevent this from crushing the delicate confidence you've nurtured for weeks, months, or even years? Explain to them that losing is part of the game and shift their focus on what went well during the game and the fact that it was fun overall. Just because the scoreboard wasn't in their favor when the time was over doesn't mean that there were no moments to acknowledge and celebrate during the game.

**Elementary Schoolers (5-10 Years)**

Now, your child's understanding of the world, confidence, and how it makes you feel is much more advanced. It means you can improve your approach in this regard too.

**Step 1: Positive Affirmations**

Does your child ask questions like, "Why am I such a loser?" or make statements like "I suck at..."? Such comments and questions express negative self-talk out loud. It is an indication of what your child is saying to themselves in their minds. Maybe you are familiar with how unkind we can be to ourselves when things don't work out as we've hoped or planned. Combat this by encouraging your child rather express positive statements about themselves. These would be statements like "I am good at helping others." or "I am friendly." As an art project, you can even make bracelets from paper, making these statements to make positive affirmations more real for them.

**Step 2: Let Mistakes Happen**

Mistakes happen to all of us, but whether a mistake is a lesson or a conviction mostly depends on your approach. Hammering on mistakes or failing to let go of past mistakes can crush your kids' confidence. Instead, explain that mistakes happen, we all make them, but we have to learn from them and then discuss with your child what they think they can do better next time.

**Step 3: Be Encouraging**

Who is your cheerleader? Are you your child's cheerleader? I guess we don't necessarily need a cheerleader in life, but it makes life a lot easier and way more fun. So, how can you be your child's cheerleader? Quite simply rely on the fact that kids can be playing on the other side of the room, but the moment they hear you mention their names while in conversation with someone else, like your partner or friends, their radar goes into high alert, and they can listen to every word you say. So, say something nice about them, not to them in this case. For example, express to your partner how proud you are of your son for helping you today, or tell your friend how well your daughter is doing at school. They'll listen. They won't hear you call them to do something when they are two steps away, but they will hear you make such statements in their absence, trust me.

**Step 4: Watch Your Words!**

Yes, you know it by now; they watch your every move and listen to every word you say. So, you have to be the perfect model all the time. Tough job, but the impact of portraying the behavior you desire rather than telling them what to do is just so much that it can't be overseen. Therefore, you need to watch your words and how you say things, never to give your confidence a blow.

**Step 5: Set Goals, But Start Small**

Setting and achieving goals is a fantastic boost for your confidence. Therefore, it is the perfect way to create opportunities to work on your child's confidence. But, if you're going to set goals that they can't achieve, repeated failure will only break their spirit. Therefore, yes, please set goals but be sure they are small enough for them to achieve them.

### Step 6: Focus on Their Strengths

I want you to take a clear white sheet of paper and then make a dot with a black marker somewhere on the paper. Done? What do you see? By far, the majority will tell me they see a black dot but fail to mention the white paper, which overshadows the dot's size. Unfortunately, that is how we treat our strengths compared to our weaknesses, and we carry this habit over to our kids too. If you find yourself hammering on that one thing they did wrong, change your perspective and start to elaborate on the many strengths your little one has. Whatever your focus on in their lives is what will accumulate.

### Step 7: Always Celebrate the Wins

Small wins lead to large accomplishments, and the more you celebrate these wins and give recognition for what was achieved, the greater the power becomes of these wins. Therefore, our home celebrates every accomplishment according to the size of the achievement. For example, a small success may mean having a scoop of ice cream on a week's night, while a big win means eating out at our favorite pizza place as a family.

## Middle Schoolers (10+)

Your child is now moving to the doorstep of adulthood. The next steps will help you to support them to grow into confident adults.

### Step 1: Quotes

Give quotes a place in your home and watch the way you bring your kids up. I still remember some of the quotes my mom often used to encourage us as kids. As quotes are such short nuggets of wisdom, they are easy to remember and become guiding lights on your journey. Examples of easy-to-remember but still powerful quotes are, "Believe you can, and you're halfway there," from Theodore Roosevelt, "You yourself, as much as anybody in the entire universe, deserves your love and affection" from Buddha. Or perhaps, "The most beautiful thing you can wear is confidence," from Blake Lively (3 Fun Ways to Teach Self-Esteem to Kids, 2019).

**Step 2: "What Do You Think?"**

Get your child's opinion and ask them what they would think or do if they were in your shoes. Of course, you don't have to pose such a question when it comes to serious adult matters, but your tween is far more aware of what is going on in your home than you may think, and they might be able to come up with advice from a fresh approach, and it will boost their confidence.

**Step 3: Don't Aim for Perfection**

Teach your kids early on that while perfection may appear to be the ideal in life, you get far more done by celebrating progress. Sure, the search for perfection can guide you along the way, but obsessing over overachieving it will only crush your spirit and stall your progress.

**Step 4: Have They Found Their Passion?**

Help your kids find their passion. Some children already know early on what they enjoy and even what they want to do one day. Others just take a bit longer. Trying several things to see what you like is the best way to determine your passion. Once you get the wheels rolling, it is much easier to change direction, so create opportunities for your child to get their wheels rolling so that they can direct it toward their passion. Knowing your passion gives you purpose, and purpose brings confidence in life.

**Step 5: Never Compare**

The best rule to follow in parenting is often, "Do unto others as you want them to do unto you." It can be so easy to compare one kid with another in those moments of frustration, but do you like to be compared to someone else? Especially if it is only done to show you where you fall short. Surely not, so resist the urge to do it to your kids. You don't like the feeling, and neither do they, so stop crushing their confidence in this manner if this is something you are guilty of.

**Step 6: Let Them Own Up**

When you make mistakes, own up to what you've done wrong and come up with ways to fix it. Most people consider taking responsibility for your actions a burden, but it is not. On the contrary, it is the only way to live freely and confidently. So, encourage your kids to own up to their mistakes, help them find solutions, and see how they thrive once the mess is resolved.

**Step 7: Keep Your Expectations Realistic**

Setting expectations is like setting goals. It must be achievable; otherwise, it only leads to frustration and disappointment. When you set expectations for your child, be sure to clearly communicate them so that they understand what you want from them and make sure your expectations are achievable.

Let's jump straight into activities to help your kids realize how awesome they are to boost their confidence.

## ACTIVITIES

### Babies

***Repeat & Repeat***

Your little one has to discover the entire world, and that takes time. They'll have to explore the same things over and over to familiarize themselves with as much detail as possible. What can you do to help them? Be patient and encourage this behavior, as it will give them the certainty and confidence that they are doing the right thing.

### Toddlers

***The Compliment Jar***

Getting compliments is quite dandy, and it gives your confidence a boost. Yet, the power of compliments becomes so much more if it is in writing. When you see your kids do something right, scribble it onto a piece of paper and put it in the compliments jar. Every kid can have a different color of paper, and they'll be able to see how their notes increase. You can open this jar occasionally and read it to the entire family.

### Preschoolers

***Catch That Compliment!***

This is a fun ball game starting with you throwing the ball to the first kid in a circle. Then, when they catch the ball, you sincerely compliment them. After that, this child needs to throw the ball to any other kid to catch, and when they do, the one throwing the ball must give the child who caught it a sincere compliment, and so it continues.

*Can You Serve the Snack?*

After completing a multi-step challenge, this task will increase your child's sense of accomplishment. In this case, the challenge is to prepare and serve a snack for the family to serve. They are free to decide what and how they want to serve, but they need to plan every aspect of the process.

## Elementary Schoolers

*Create a Box of Memories*

Your child receives awards, recognition notes, and certificates throughout the year. Create a memory box where they can store all memories of things that matter to them and serve as a testimony of how they overcame hardship. At certain times, or when they feel down, this box and its contents remind them what they can do to boost their confidence.

*5 Things I Like About Me*

While what others think of us has a huge impact on our lives, we also need to be our own cheerleaders at times. This exercise will help your child to boost their confidence. It is a writing exercise, and your kid must list five things they like about themselves. This list can go up on a wall or a mirror and can even change as time passes, but your child must recognize the things they like about themselves.

## Middle Schoolers

### *Make a Wins List*

The exercise is much like the memory box and consists of creating a list of all your child's wins during the year. Initially, you can help them to start this list, but later, they need to keep it updated. Remember, small wins are still wins, and no accomplishment is too small to list.

### *Your Manifesto*

Life is much less daunting if we have a plan. So, help your child to create a manifesto in which they state what they want from life, what type of friends they want to have, what kind of friends they want to be, and how they want others to see them. Be flexible and add as much information as possible to guide them along. You and your child can collaborate on this exercise, but they must do most of the work themselves.

## In Conclusion

The level of confidence your child portrays in life will largely impact the quality of their relationships, success, financial state, and happiness, to name only some of the areas influenced by confidence. As this is such an essential part of their being, it is never too early to encourage them to be more confident. While a lack of confidence will impact their social life negatively, being overconfident will also not serve them well, as nobody likes to hang around with a show-off. Therefore, while you should boost their confidence, do so authentically. Create opportunities to do it, but don't praise your child for things they didn't achieve.

And this is where we reach the point where we need to wrap it all up. So please proceed with me to the conclusion to tie up any loose ends.

# CONCLUSION

You've noticed that your child is struggling to make friends, is always wandering alone on the playground, or seems that they make friends but can maintain lasting relationships. It is surely a reason to be concerned, as you also know that being social is about far more than merely having a lot of friends. Your child's ability to be social will impact every aspect of their future, happiness, and success. However, many factors play in their ability to be social, which means that there is a lot you can do at home to help them overcome obstacles keeping them from being social.

Taking on the activities and fun games in this book will improve their social skills and bring added benefits as they will help your child in many other areas of life. This book shared many insights and their relevance in every stage of development. It also equipped you with a toolbox loaded with helpful tricks to help your child. It is a book you can refer to whenever your child ages into a new stage and a way to monitor their progress.

I hope you've enjoyed this journey, feel enriched by all the knowledge and tips you've gained, and enjoy increased confidence in your ability to help your child become their best version.

Now, there is only one thing left to do: Change how your child perceives the world!

# LEAVE A REVIEW

As an independent author with a small marketing budget, reviews are my livelihood on this platform. If you enjoyed the book, I would really appreciate it if you left your honest feedback. You can do so by visiting the link or scanning the QR code below. I love hearing from my readers, and I personally read every single review. Please share your positive experiences and help other parents to access this toolbox too.

**https://geni.us/SocialSkillsforKids**

# REFERENCES


Ackerman, C. E. (2019, July 20). *40 Kindness activities & empathy worksheets for students and adults.* Positive Psychology. https://positivepsychology.com/kindness-activities-empathy-worksheets/

Barrington, K. (2022, May 27). *The importance of friendships for grade school students.* Public School Review. https://www.publicschoolreview.com/blog/the-importance-of-friendships-for-grade-school-students

Bayless, K. (2022, May 26). *How to help your child make friends.* Parents. https://www.parents.com/kids/development/friends/making-friends/

Bell, S. (2016, May 19). *Developing self-confidence from birth to 12 months.* Zero to Tree. https://www.zerotothree.org/resource/developing-self-confidence-from-birth-to-12-months/

Bharatan, N. (2022, December 16). 20 *Creative friendship activities for toddlers & preschoolers.* Mom Junction. https://www.momjunction.com/articles/friendship-activities-for-toddlers-preschoolers_00779599/

Bounds, L. A. (n.d.). *6 Fun decision making games for kids.* Leaps and Bounds. https://leapsandboundsschool.com/6-fun-decision-making-games/

Byrd, F. (2022, December 8). *Preschooler emotional development.* WebMD. https://www.webmd.com/parenting/preschooler-emotional-development

Centers, K. L. (n.d.). *Teach good decision-making skills and say goodbye to power struggles.* KinderCare. https://www.kindercare.com/content-hub/articles/2016/december/let-your-child-make-her-own-choices-and-put-the-power-struggles-behind-you

Chambers, Y. S. (n.d.). *Best guide for teaching kids the decision making process steps.* Kiddie Matters. https://www.kiddiematters.com/problem-solving-activity-free-printable/

Chanda, S. (2021, March 4). *55 Best "raising children" quotes that are really relatable.* Kidadl. https://kidadl.com/quotes/best-raising-children-quotes-that-are-really-relatable

Cherry, K. (2022, November 7). *What is self-esteem*? Verywell Mind. https://www.verywellmind.com/what-is-self-esteem-2795868

Colino, S., & Broadwell, L. (2015, June 11). *A parent's guide for how to deal with bullies.* Parents. https://www.parents.com/kids/problems/bullying/bully-proof-your-child-how-to-deal-with-bullies/

*Communication games for middle school kids: Its importance and examples.* (2021, February 24). The Real School. https://therealschool.in/blog/communication-games-for-middle-school-kids-its-importance-and-examples/

Conway, S. (2018, August 26). *How to teach your child emotional regulation skills in 6 steps.* Mindful Little Minds Psychology. https://www.mindfullittleminds.com/help-your-child-manage-emotions/

Cornwall, G. (2020, November 30). *How understanding middle school friendships can help students with ups and downs.* KQED. https://www.kqed.org/mindshift/57010/how-understanding-middle-school-friendships-can-help-students

Cortese, R. (2016, February 2). *Helping toddlers expand language skills.* Child Mind Institute. https://childmind.org/article/helping-toddlers-expand-their-language-skills/

Crider, C. (2020, December 8). *8 Self-soothing techniques to help your baby.* Healthline. https://www.healthline.com/health/baby/self-soothing-baby#leave-in-crib

Cullins, A. (n.d.-a). *25 things you can do right now to build a child's confidence.* Big Life Journal. https://biglifejournal.com/blogs/blog/child-confidence

Cullins, A. (n.d.-b). *Key strategies to teach children empathy (Sorted by age).* Big Life Journal. https://biglifejournal.com/blogs/blog/key-strategies-teach-children-empathy

*Decision making games for students.* (n.d.). Decision Making Games. https://decision makinggames.jimdosite.com/

*Decision-making techniques for children.* (n.d.). Family Education. https://www.fami lyeducation.com/kids/responsibilities/decision-making-techniques-children

Dewar, G. (n.d.). *How to help kids make friends: 12 evidence-based tips.* Parenting Science. https://parentingscience.com/kids-make-friends/

Dewar, G. (2020). *Teaching empathy: Evidence-based tips for fostering empathic awareness in children.* Parenting Science. https://parentingscience.com/teaching-empathy-tips/

Dinkin, K. (2023, January 4). *15 Activities on friendship for middle school learners.* Teaching Expertise. https://www.teachingexpertise.com/classroom-ideas/activities-on-friendship-for-middle-school/

*Do you know the 3 types of self-esteem?* (2015, November 23). Exploring Your Mind. https://exploringyourmind.com/know-3-types-self-esteem/

*Easier to build strong children than to repair broken adults.* (2015, October 7). Keen for God. http://www.keenforgod.com/2015/10/07/easier-to-build-strong-chil dren-than-to-repair-broken-adults/

Ehmke, R. (2022, June 8). *Tips for communicating with your teen.* Child Mind Institute. https://childmind.org/article/tips-communicating-with-teen/

*8 Ways to boost your child's Confidence and Self-esteem.* (n.d.). Health Hub. https://www.healthhub.sg/live-healthy/439/healthy_selfesteem_for_your_child

*Emotions and play: babies.* (n.d.). Raising Children Network. https://raisingchildren.net.au/babies/play-learning/play-baby-development/emotions-play-babies

*Empathy for beginners: when do babies tune in to others' thoughts and feelings?* (2019, April). National Childbirth Trust. https://www.nct.org.uk/baby-toddler/toddler-tantrums-and-tricky-behaviour/empathy-for-beginners-when-do-babies-tune-others-thoughts-and-feelings

*5 Activities for building empathy in your students.* (2017, February 21). Brookes Publishing. https://blog.brookespublishing.com/5-activities-for-building-empathy-in-your-students/

*5 Tips for cultivating empathy.* (2018, October 13). Making Caring Common. https://mcc.gse.harvard.edu/resources-for-families/5-tips-cultivating-empathy

Foley, M. (2022, August 9). *How to build your child's confidence and self-esteem.* Child Development Institute. https://childdevelopmentinfo.com/parenting/how-to-build-your-childs-confidence-and-self-esteem/

*Forcing toddlers to apologize doesn't teach empathy—Here's what does.* (2021, January 12). The Everymom. https://theeverymom.com/how-to-teach-empathy-to-toddlers/

Fritzgerald, M. (2022, March 21). *Easy activities that teach kids empathy.* Tinkergarten. https://tinkergarten.com/blog/easy-day-to-day-ways-to-teach-kids-affective-empathy

Gillespie, C. (2018, October 1). *10 apps to help kids control their emotions.* Mashable. https://mashable.com/article/apps-kids-mindfulness-control-emotions

*Giving children choices.* (2017). PennState Extension. https://extension.psu.edu/programs/betterkidcare/early-care/tip-pages/all/giving-children-choices

Gordon, S. (2020, August 25). *10 Ways to discipline your child for bullying others.* Verywell Family. https://www.verywellfamily.com/ways-discipline-child-for-bullying-others-460520

Group, L. S. (2018, October 31). *5 Ways to improve young children's Decision-making.* Life Skills Group. https://www.lifeskillsgroup.com.au/blog/5-ways-to-improve-young-childrens-decision-making

Heger, E. (2022, December 12). *6 essential tips for helping your kids develop empathy, according to child psychologists.* Insider. https://www.insider.com/guides/parenting/how-to-teach-empathy-to-kids

*Help your baby learn to talk.* (2020, August 7). NHS. https://www.nhs.uk/conditions/baby/babys-development/play-and-learning/help-your-baby-learn-to-talk/

*Help your child recognize the signs of bullying.* (2022). Pacer. https://www.pacer.org/publications/bullypdf/BP-2.pdf

*Helping children learn decision-making skills.* (n.d.). https://static1.squarespace.com/static/5a7db7ac2278e79460f1b2c7/t/619bc05f05b09040778641fd/1637597279175/helping+children+learn+decision+making+skills.pdf

*Helping children learn how to manage emotions.* (2018, March 5). Psych Central. https://psychcentral.com/blog/helping-children-learn-how-to-manage-emotions#1

*Helping kids deal with bullies.* (n.d.). Kids Health. https://kidshealth.org/en/parents/bullies.html

Henry, S. (n.d.). *How to build your preschooler's self-esteem.* Baby Center. https://www.babycenter.com/child/development/how-to-build-your-preschoolers-self-esteem_64036

Hester, J. (2015, April 13). *Age-by-age advice for teaching empathy.* Scholastic. https://www.scholastic.com/parents/family-life/parent-child/age-age-advice-teaching-empathy.html

Higuera, V. (2020, March 25). *How to Teach Your Toddler to Talk.* Healthline. https://www.healthline.com/health/how-to-teach-toddler-to-talk

*How to make friends.* (2021, May). Pregnancy Birth & Baby. https://www.pregnancybirthbaby.org.au/how-children-make-friends

Howard, J. (2023, January 26). *Kids who need a little help to make friends.* Child Mind Institute. https://childmind.org/article/kids-who-need-a-little-help-to-make-friends/

Hurley, K. (2019, September 13). *Helping kids communicate with one another.* PBS Kids for Parents. https://www.pbs.org/parents/thrive/helping-kids-communicate-with-one-another

*Importance of teaching kids decision-making skills in early childhood.* (n.d.). Rainforest Learning Centre. https://rainforestlearningcentre.ca/the-importance-of-teaching-kids-decision-making-skills-in-early-childhood/

*Is my child a bully?* (n.d.). Bullies Out. https://bulliesout.com/need-support/parents/bullying/is-my-child-a-bully/

Jamie. (2014, August 11). *Back to School Scattergories Free Printable.* The Crafting Chicks. https://thecraftingchicks.com/back-to-school-scattergories-free-printable

Jules. (2019, August 2). *How do young children learn to make decisions?* Tapestry. https://tapestry.info/2019/08/02/how-do-young-children-learn-to-make-decisions.html

Katz, B. (2023, January 25). *My child is a bully: What should I do?* Child Mind Institute. https://childmind.org/article/what-to-do-if-your-child-is-bullying/#communicate

Kokoski, C. (2020, December 26). *A love letter to my middle school bullies*. Medium. https://medium.com/hello-love/a-love-letter-to-my-middle-school-bullies-dc28ec92b877

Kristenson, S. (2022, July 6). *15 Self esteem activities for kindergarteners*. Happier Human. https://www.happierhuman.com/self-esteem-kindergarteners/

LaRowe, M. (2012, September 13). *5 Ways to prepare your child for bullies*. Momtastic. https://www.momtastic.com/teens-and-tweens/398087-5-ways-to-prepare-your-child-for-bullies/

Lee, K. (2021, October 8). *9 Ways to build more self-esteem in your child*. Verywell Family. https://www.verywellfamily.com/ways-to-build-strong-self-esteem-in-your-child-3953464

Lehman, J. (n.d.). *Is Your Child Being Bullied? 9 Steps You Can Take as a Parent*. Empowering Parents. https://www.empoweringparents.com/article/is-your-child-being-bullied-9-steps-you-can-take-as-a-parent/

*Lesson seven: There's nothing better than a good friend*. (n.d.). Healthy Sexuality

Line up game. (n.d.). Activity Village. https://www.activityvillage.co.uk/the-line-up-game

Lynch, M. (2018, August 24). *7 ways to teach your child to be a good friend*. The Edvocate. https://www.theedadvocate.org/7-ways-teach-child-good-friend/

Lyness, D. (2018, July). *Your child's self-esteem*. Kids Health. https://kidshealth.org/en/parents/self-esteem.html

Maguire, C. (2019, May 29). *4 Tips for when your teen gives you the silent treatment*. Your Teen Magazine. https://yourteenmag.com/teenager-school/teenager-middle-school/communication-skills-middle-school

Maguire, C. (2020, December 12). *Teaching empathy to children: 5 Tips from a child care expert*. Mind Body Green. https://www.mindbodygreen.com/articles/teaching-empathy-to-children-tips-from-child-care-expert

Mar, Z. D. (2022, January 10). *7 Teaching empathy activities for middle schoolers*. HMH. https://www.hmhco.com/blog/teaching-empathy-activities-for-middle-schoolers

Markham, L. (2013, July 5). *5 Steps to help kids learn to control their emotions*. Psychology Today. https://www.psychologytoday.com/us/blog/peaceful-parents-happy-kids/201307/5-steps-help-kids-learn-control-their-emotions

Mead, S. (n.d.). *6 Self esteem activities to help your child develop confidence*. Whitby School. https://www.whitbyschool.org/passionforlearning/6-self-esteem-activities-to-help-your-child-develop-confidence

Miller, G. (2023, January 19). *Helping kids make decisions*. Child Mind Institute. https://childmind.org/article/helping-kids-make-decisions/

Miller, K. (2019, May 21). *39 Communication games and activities for kids, teens, and students*. Positive Psychology. https://positivepsychology.com/communication-activities-adults-students/

Morin, A. (n.d.-a). *6 ways to help your preschooler connect with other kids*. Understood. https://www.understood.org/en/articles/6-ways-to-help-your-preschooler-connect-with-other-kids

Morin, A. (n.d.-b). *8 ways to help your middle-schooler connect with other kids*. Understood. https://www.understood.org/en/articles/8-ways-to-help-your-middle-schooler-connect-with-other-kids

Morin, A. (n.d.-c). *10 ways to help your grade-schooler connect with other kids*. Understood. https://www.understood.org/en/articles/10-ways-to-help-your-grade-schooler-connect-with-other-kids

Morin, A. (2021, April 25). *How to help overly emotional kids deal with their big feelings*. Verywell Family. https://www.verywellfamily.com/how-to-help-an-overly-emotional-child-4157594

Morin, A. (2022, June 16). *The best way to make friends is to be a good friend*. Verywell Family. https://www.verywellfamily.com/how-to-teach-your-child-to-be-a-good-friend-4007427

Muriel, C. (2022, April 14). *25 Fun friendship activities for kids*. Very Special Tales. https://veryspecialtales.com/friendship-activities-for-kids/

Myers, R. C. (2023, March 16). *11 tips on building self-esteem in children*. Today's Parent. https://www.todaysparent.com/family/parenting/how-to-build-your-childs-self-esteem/

Nair, A. (2018, December 13). *8 Activities for language development in babies up to 6 months*. Firstcry Parenting. https://parenting.firstcry.com/articles/8-activities-for-language-development-in-babies-up-to-6-months/

O'Donnell, L. M. (2018, June). *Teaching your child self-control*. Kids Health. https://kidshealth.org/en/parents/self-control.html

Oey, K. W. (n.d.). *How to develop age appropriate decision making skills in your kids*. The Asian Parent. https://sg.theasianparent.com/age-appropriate-decision-making

Parlakian, R. (2016, February 1). *How to help your child develop empathy*. Zero to Three. https://www.zerotothree.org/resource/how-to-help-your-child-develop-empathy/

Pelini, S. (n.d.). *An age-by-age guide to helping kids manage emotions*. The Gottman Institute. https://www.gottman.com/blog/age-age-guide-helping-kids-manage-emotions/

Pelini, S. (2017, July 17). *Why and how to talk to kids about emotions*. Raising-Independent-Kids. https://raising-independent-kids.com/talk-kids-emotions/

Ph.D., J. S. (2021, June 11). *Anger management for kids: 14 Best activities & worksheets*.

Positive Psychology. https://positivepsychology.com/anger-management-kids/#strategies

Pincus, D. (n.d.). *My child is out of control: How to teach kids to manage emotions.* Empowering Parents. https://www.empoweringparents.com/article/my-child-is-out-of-control-how-to-teach-kids-to-manage-emotions/

*Preschool bullying: helping your child.* (2022, November 28). Raising Children Network. https://raisingchildren.net.au/preschoolers/behaviour/bullying/preschool-bullying-helping

Preschoolers making friends. (2020, November 23). Raising Children Network. https://raisingchildren.net.au/preschoolers/behaviour/friends-siblings/preschoolers-making-friends

Price, S. (2011, September 28). *Raising good decision makers: Helping kids learn to make decisions.* ParentMap. https://www.parentmap.com/article/helping-kids-learn-to-make-decisions

*Quote by Neil deGrasse Tyson.* (n.d.). Goodreads. https://www.goodreads.com/quotes/562509-we-spend-the-first-year-of-a-child-s-life-teaching

Raising Children Network. (2021, May 20). *Self-regulation in young children.* Raising Children Network. https://raisingchildren.net.au/toddlers/behaviour/understanding-behaviour/self-regulation

Rauch, C. A. (n.d.). *How to help your child make friends.* BabyCenter. https://www.babycenter.com/child/development/how-to-help-your-child-make-friends_64133

Rebbapragada, S. (2022, November 29). *100+ Best and cute quotes about friendship for kids.* MomJunction. https://www.momjunction.com/articles/best-funny-quotes-about-friendship-for-kids_00680631/

*Recognising and managing emotions.* (n.d.). Skills You Need. https://www.skillsyouneed.com/ps/managing-emotions.html

Reed, S. (2021, February 1). *15 inspiring parenting quotes to live by.* Care.com. https://www.care.com/c/inspirational-parenting-quotes/

Reilly, K. M. (2022, December 29). *10 Ways to boost baby's language development.* Parents. https://www.parents.com/baby/development/talking/signs-of-talking/

Rogers, L. (2022, December 5). *How to help your toddler make friends.* What to Expect. https://www.whattoexpect.com/toddler/how-to-help-your-toddler-make-friends.aspx

Rosbach, M. (2020, July 1). *Books about friendship for babies and toddlers.* Brightly. https://www.readbrightly.com/books-on-friendship-babies-toddlers/

Rouse, M. H. (2023, January 19). *How can we help kids with self-regulation?* Child Mind Institute. https://childmind.org/article/can-help-kids-self-regulation/

Rymanowicz, K. (2018, December 3). *Self-regulation for infants and toddlers.* Early

Childhood Development. https://www.canr.msu.edu/news/self-regulation-for-infants-and-toddlers

Saltz, G. (2023, January 24). *How to arm your child against bullying.* Child Mind Institute. https://childmind.org/article/how-to-arm-your-child-against-bullying/

Sauber, T. (2022, January 18). *16 Activities to stimulate emotional development in children.* Positive Psychology. https://positivepsychology.com/emotional-development-activities/

*School-age friendships: how to support them.* (2022, December 19). Raising Children Network. https://raisingchildren.net.au/school-age/connecting-communicating/connecting/supporting-friendships

*Self-esteem in children: 1-8 years.* (2021, May 7). Raising Children Network. https://raisingchildren.net.au/toddlers/behaviour/understanding-behaviour/about-self-esteem

*7 Ways to Foster Self-esteem and Resilience in All Learners.* (2017, November 7). Brookes Publishing. https://blog.brookespublishing.com/7-ways-to-foster-self-esteem-and-resilience-in-all-learners/

*6 Ways to help your baby self-soothe and find calm.* (2022, November 18). Cleveland Clinic. https://health.clevelandclinic.org/self-soothing-techniques/

Skurat, K. (2022, December 27). *Are you suppressing your emotions or in control of them?* Calmerry Blog. https://us.calmerry.com/blog/self-care/are-you-suppressing-your-emotions-or-in-control-of-them/

*Simple and fun game to practice making decisions.* (2016, October 13). Encourage Play. https://www.encourageplay.com/blog/a-simple-and-fun-game-to-practice-making-decisions

Stanford Children's Health. (n.d.). *Age-appropriate speech and language milestones.* Stanford Medicine Children's Health. https://www.stanfordchildrens.org/en/topic/default?id=age-appropriate-speech-and-language-milestones-90-P02170

Stutman, M. (n.d.). *Great empathy quotes for kids and students.* InspireMyKids. https://inspiremykids.com/great-empathy-quotes-kids-students-children/

Suttie, J. (2016, June 10). *Seven ways to foster empathy in kids.* Greater Good. https://greatergood.berkeley.edu/article/item/seven_ways_to_foster_empathy_in_kids

Sutton, J. (n.d.-a). *Building our feelings vocabulary.* Positive Psychology. https://positive.b-cdn.net/wp-content/uploads/2021/06/Building-Our-Feelings-Vocabulary.pdf

Sutton, J. (n.d.-b). *Make a manifesto for you.* https://positive.b-cdn.net/wp-content/uploads/2020/09/Make-a-Manifesto-for-YOU.pdf

Sutton, J. (2020, October 1). *Self-esteem for kids: 30+ Counseling tools & activities.*

Positive Psychology. https://positivepsychology.com/self-esteem-for-children/#activities

*Talking and play: toddlers.* (n.d.). Raising Children Network. https://raisingchildren.net.au/toddlers/play-learning/play-toddler-development/talking-play-toddlers

Tarango, T. (n.d.). *Preparing for school: 4 Strategies to prevent bullying.* Dilly's Tree House. https://www.dillystreehouse.com/bullying/

*Teaching guide: Friendship.* (n.d.). Good Character. https://www.goodcharacter.com/middle_school/friendship/

*10 Activities for teaching young children about emotions.* (2021, January 26). Brookes Blog. https://blog.brookespublishing.com/10-activities-for-teaching-young-children-about-emotions/

*10 Fun communication games for toddlers.* (n.d.). Wee Talkers. https://www.weetalkers.com/blog/10-communication-games-for-toddlers

*10 Ways to Teach Your Children to Make Wise Decisions.* (n.d.). All Pro Dad. https://www.allprodad.com/10-ways-teach-children-make-wise-decisions/

*3 Fun Ways to Teach Self Esteem to Kids.* (2019, May 3). The Counseling Teacher. https://thecounselingteacher.com/2019/05/3-fun-ways-to-teach-self-esteem-to-kids.html

*Tips on learning to talk.* (2016, February 25). Zero to Three. https://www.zerotothree.org/resource/tips-on-learning-to-talk/

*12 Tips for Raising confident kids.* (2022, December 19). Child Mind Institute. https://childmind.org/article/12-tips-raising-confident-kids/

UNICEF. (n.d.). *How to communicate effectively with your young child.* Unicef. https://www.unicef.org/parenting/child-care/9-tips-for-better-communication

VanClay, M. (2022). *The caring child: How to teach empathy (ages 3 to 4).* BabyCenter. https://www.babycenter.com/child/parenting-strategies/the-caring-child-how-to-teach-empathy-ages-3-to-4_65717

Walters Wright, L. (n.d.). *10 Ways to help your grade schooler's communication skills.* Understood. https://www.understood.org/en/articles/10-ways-to-improve-your-grade-schoolers-communication-skills

Watts, A. (n.d.). *7 Confidence-building activities for kids.* IMOM. https://www.imom.com/7-confidence-building-activities-kids/

*Ways to help your child make friends in school.* (2021, April 6). Cleveland Clinic. https://health.clevelandclinic.org/ways-help-child-make-friends-school/

WeAreTeachers Staff. (n.d.). *Teach students about healthy friendships in preparation for middle school.* We Are Teachers. https://www.weareteachers.com/healthy-friendships/

*What are decision-making skills?* (n.d.). Twink. https://www.twinkl.com.ph/teaching-wiki/decision-making-skills

*What to do if your child is a bully*. (n.d.). Stomp out Bullying. https://www.stompoutbullying.org/what-do-if-your-child-bully

Wong, R. R. (2020, July 4). *7 ways to help your child make good decisions*. Smart Parents. https://www.smartparents.sg/child/social-life-skills/7-ways-help-your-child-make-good-decisions

Made in the USA
Columbia, SC
15 November 2023